A John Catt Publication

The Mr Salles Guide to

100% in AQA

English Language
GCSE

First Published 2017

by John Catt Educational Ltd,
12 Deben Mill Business Centre, Old Maltings Approach,
Melton, Woodbridge IP12 1BL
Tel: +44 (0) 1394 389850 Fax: +44 (0) 1394 386893
Email: enquiries@johncatt.com
Website: www.johncatt.com

© **2017 Dominic Salles**

Opinions expressed in this publication are those of the contributors
and are not necessarily those of the publishers or the editors.
We cannot accept responsibility for any errors or omissions.

ISBN: 9781-911382-25-6

Set and designed by Theoria Design Limited
www.theoriadesign.com

Printed and bound in Great Britain

Contents

Introduction

Thank you and congratulations for buying this guide.

You have chosen to begin with high expectations. That's why 100% is in the title: The Mr. Salles Guide to **100%** in AQA GCSE English Language. This detail is important.

Is this guide still relevant to every student? Yes. It's just that most students don't think they can get an A or A* in the old GCSE nor, in the new exam, this exam, a 7 or 8, let alone the new 'beyond A*' grade of 9. But I think you can and I've written this guide to help you do that. I'm a teacher who loves teaching, and the joy of teaching is helping students to reach their potential. This is why I want you to aim high.

If you want to see what teaching that makes you get 100% looks like, you can visit my YouTube channel, Mr Salles Teaches English. My videos and this guide will make you think hard.

This guide does the same thing, but makes it quicker for you. It takes dozens of English lessons you have had, and compresses them into about 3 hours. It will teach you more than you learned in all those English lessons, and that is a promise. No other teacher will be teaching you the stuff in this guide.

Why this guide is better than school

Let's pause a minute and think about your school. The balance of probability is that you have a good English teacher, and your class has about 28 students in it. However great your teacher, he or she won't be able to teach you all well. There are too many of you, with different starting points, and different needs. But if you use this guide, it will teach you how to teach yourself. I'll show you many techniques to make you brilliant at English, which will last you for life, beyond your GCSE. Again, this is why I teach.

This guide is also about the exam. Possibly as many as 50% of the marks available are for exam technique. Exams are always stupid in this way, in the same way that crowds are often stupid, even if they are made up of very clever people. An exam has to cover so many different skills, that it becomes very artificial. This is not the examiner's fault, it is just that exams are not trying to test just you, but an enormously large crowd of around 500,000 students.

This is also important, because with my English degree, my 24 years of teaching English, and a lifetime of reading every single day, I couldn't get 100% on this exam when the sample papers first came out. I know, because I sat the papers before I looked at the mark schemes. I always do this because it teaches me which marks have nothing to do with English, but everything to do with the artificiality of exams. I'll show you how to get these marks too, because I want you to be able to get 100%.

How do I know this works? Well, I've had over a million views on YouTube, and regularly get students telling me they got A* because of me. But you could argue that in a million views, that's bound to happen with lots of students; it isn't proof my advice is any good. So how else do I know my advice will work?

I am still a real teacher, in a normal comprehensive school. Every year, students predicted grades C and B get A and A* in my class. And obviously, those predicted higher get A and A*. Hopefully you've seen my teaching on YouTube, at Mr Salles Teaches English, and are well on your way to success already.

Why this guide is more useful than any other guide

Each question begins with '**just tell me what to do**'. That's 10 questions, and 10 pages. If you are in a hurry, learn just those pages and you are nearly ready. No other guide summarises its advice for you this way.

Each question has a section, '**so, what does the examiner really want?**' which digs deep into the mark scheme. The writers of other guides don't actually sit the exam under timed conditions to find out what you need to do. Often this means they give you the wrong advice. I do all the questions under exam conditions so I know what the issues are, and so my advice is spot on.

Each question has a 100% and a beyond 100% answer, so that you can learn to be an expert, not just in the GCSE English exam, but also in preparation for A level, or in becoming a writer yourself. No other guide does that, either.

Only 2 out of the 10 questions are writing questions, so most guides spend too little time preparing you for the writing skills. This is a real problem, as those 2 questions count for 50% of your whole GCSE. This guide will show you how to become a writer, and the writing questions will become, not just easy, but a part of the exam you look forward to. And you know no other guide does that!

A man walks into a bar with a lizard on his shoulder.
"I'd like a pint, a whisky for Tiny," says the man.
Curiosity gets the better of the barman.
"Why do you call him Tiny?"
"Because he's my newt."

Chapter 1: How to Use the Sample Papers

You can find the specimen papers, papers 1 and 2, on the AQA website at:
http://www.aqa.org.uk/subjects/english/gcse/english-language-8700/assessment-resources

You should practice using these in the following ways:

- Do each question separately – read part of my guide on one question. Then just do that question on the specimen papers.

- Use the marks scheme to grade yourself.

- Use my guide, with the greater number of skills, and work out which ones you've used, and which ones you have to master.

- Answer the question again, with either, or both, of the mark scheme and this guide open at the same time. Your aim in 'cheating' in this way is to write an answer that scores 100%.

- After a few days, do the same question again, under exam conditions, with no cheating. Can you still remember how to get 100%? Can you do it in the time limit?

- If your answer is too long, practise the skills I taught you for reducing its length, so it is the number of words you can write in the exam time.

- Once you have what you consider to be answers that are as close to 100% as possible, give them to your teacher to mark, or post them on Mr. Salles Teaches English. Remember, just like the real examiners, your teacher and I might grade your answer differently – that isn't important. What is important is that you correctly judge the skills which you have included in the answer.

(You can just read the guide of course, but how will you know it is making a difference?)

Two nuns are driving through Forks, Washington, at midnight.

Suddenly, a vampire smashes onto their bonnet, and hisses at them, baring its fangs.

"Quick, Mother Superior," shouts one nun, "show him your cross!"

"Get off my F%@*g car!" she yells, crossly.

Paper 1 (50% of your GCSE)

Explorations in Creative Reading and Writing

1 Hour and 45 minutes
This paper focuses on fiction.
There will be an insert, with one fiction text from the 20th or 21st century.

Section A contains 4 questions, and covers reading. It is worth 40 marks.
Section B contains 1 question and it covers writing. It is also worth 40 marks.
The writing question will ask you to write a description or narrative.

Timing of questions

These are the marks for the questions:

Question 1	4 marks	6 minutes	2.5% of your whole GCSE
Question 2	8 marks	12 minutes	5% of your whole GCSE
Question 3	8 marks	12 minutes	5% of your whole GCSE
Question 4	20 marks	30 minutes	12.5% of your whole GCSE
Question 5	40 marks	45 minutes	25% of your whole GCSE

Exam tactics

Because you will get more and more tired as the exam goes on, you should answer the questions in reverse order. This is because each one is worth more marks than the next. You will score more marks this way. You will also get to know the texts better this way. This will feel scary, so you should try it in your mocks, or for revision. But it is by far the most logical way to approach scoring 100%.

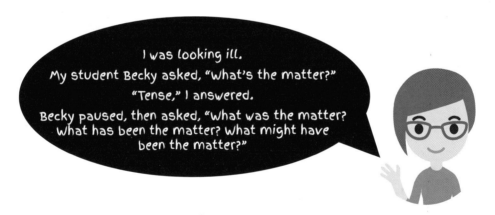

I was looking ill.
My student Becky asked, "What's the matter?"
"Tense," I answered.
Becky paused, then asked, "What was the matter? What has been the matter? What might have been the matter?"

Paper 2 (50% of your whole GCSE)

Writers' Viewpoints and Perspectives

1 hour and 45 minutes.
This paper focuses on non-fiction.
This paper will have an insert, with two texts. One will be from the 19th century, and the other will be from the 20th or 21st centuries.

Section A contains 4 questions, and covers Reading. It is worth 40 marks.
Section B contains 1 question and it covers Writing. It is also worth 40 marks.
The writing question will ask you to persuade, argue or inform.

Timing of questions

These are the marks for the questions:

Question 1	4 marks	6 minutes	2.5% of your whole GCSE
Question 2	8 marks	12 minutes	5% of your whole GCSE
Question 3	12 marks	18 minutes	7.5% of your whole GCSE
Question 4	16 marks	24 minutes	10% of your whole GCSE
Question 5	40 marks	45 minutes	25% of your whole GCSE

Exam tactics

Because you will get more and more tired as the exam goes on, you should answer the questions in reverse order. This is because each one is worth more marks than the next. You will score more marks this way. This will feel scary, so you should try it in your mocks, or for revision.

However, there is another alternative that makes reading the texts easier. The order would then be questions: 5, 1, 3, 4, 2.

In this way, you will deal with all the questions on single texts first, and then the last two questions, 4 and 2, will deal with both texts at the same time.

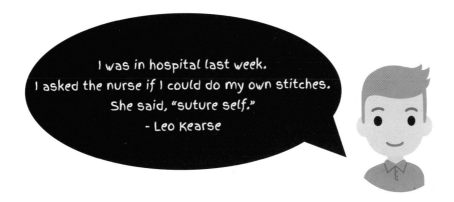

I was in hospital last week.
I asked the nurse if I could do my own stitches.
She said, "suture self."
- Leo Kearse

Reading: paper 1 and 2

This is question numbers 1 to 4 on each paper. This is what the government has told the exam boards that every student needs to be able to do to get a grade 8 in the English Language exam:

Grade 8
1.1 Critical reading and comprehension
In relation to a range of texts, to achieve grade 8, candidates will be able to:

- **Summarise** and critically **evaluate** with detailed and **perceptive** understanding
- Understand and respond with insight to explicit and **implicit meanings and viewpoints**
- Analyse and critically evaluate, with insight, detailed aspects of **language, grammar and structure**
- Substantiate their understanding and opinions with illuminating references to texts and contexts
- Make convincing and **apt links** and comparisons within and between texts

How ready are you? Take a look at the checklist below to find out:

Your Reading Checklist			
Skill	**No**	**Nearly**	**Yes**
• **Summarise and critically evaluate with detailed and perceptive understanding**			
Write a detailed summary			
• **Summarise and critically evaluate with detailed and perceptive understanding** • **Understand and respond with insight to explicit and implicit meanings and viewpoints**			
Evaluate different points of view from the same text			
Recognise an author's viewpoint			
Interpret ideas and words to work out an author's viewpoint			
• **Analyse and critically evaluate, with insight, detailed aspects of language, grammar and structure**			
Explain the effect of the writer's choice of vocabulary			
Explain the effect of the writer's choice of word order and grammar			
Explain the effect of the writer's choice of rhetorical techniques			
Explain the effect of the writer's choice of descriptive techniques			
Explain the effect of the writer's choice of paragraphs			
Explain the effect of a writer's choice of sentence types			
Explain the effect of the writer's choice of when details are revealed			
Explain the how and why the writer changes the pace of action or thought			
Explain the how and why the writer changes the focus of action or thought			
• **Substantiate their understanding and opinions with illuminating references to texts and contexts**			
Analyse short quotations			
Embed short quotations			
Include your explanation and quotation without using PEE paragraphs			
Know and recognise the 19th century attitude to childhood and schooling, Christianity, a woman's role, the rule of Empire, social injustice, the gothic genre, advances in science, impact of the theory of evolution.			
• **Make convincing and apt links and comparisons within and between texts**			
Compare writers' viewpoints			
Compare the writers' intentions			

Once you have read through this guide, come back to the checklist and see how far you have improved, and what you still have left to revise.

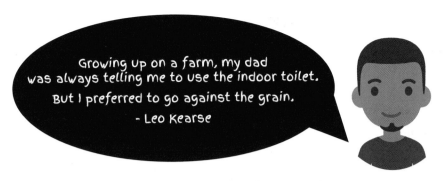

Growing up on a farm, my dad was always telling me to use the indoor toilet. But I preferred to go against the grain.
- Leo Kearse

Writing: paper 1 and paper 2 (question 5 in both papers)

1.2 Writing
To achieve grade 8, candidates will be able to:

- **Communicate with impact** and influence
- Produce **ambitious**, accomplished and **effectively-structured** texts
- Use a **wide range of well-selected sentence types** and structures and **precise vocabulary** to enhance impact
- **Spell, punctuate and use grammar accurately so that writing is virtually error-free**

How grades 8 and 9 are calculated

However, you can still get a grade 8 or 9 without these skills:

"Under the formula now proposed by Ofqual, the proportion of pupils getting a grade 7 in a subject will be divided by two, then seven percentage points will be added to reveal the proportion of pupils receiving the top grade.

For example, if 22% of pupils achieved a grade 7 in (English Language), the number would be divided by two to give 11 per cent. Seven percentage points would then be added, to give a figure of 18 per cent. This would mean (the top) 18 per cent of scorers among the grade 7 achievers would receive a grade 9."

http://schoolsweek.co.uk/ofqual-reveals-method-for-allocating-highest-grades-in-new-gcses/

Now, just imagine that no one in the country was good enough to get the level 8 skills. What would happen then? Well, the same would still apply – 18 per cent of grade 7s would still get a level 9. If this all sounds a bit bonkers, don't worry. If you concentrate on the grade 8 skills, you will easily gain a grade 7. Then you will be in with a good chance of getting a grade 8 or 9. That is why this guide is all about those grade 8 skills.

Chapter 2: What Your Teachers Don't Tell You

Before You Start

This section is about the exam as a whole. It is about how you get the right mindset to ace this exam. Much of the advice will also help you in most of your exams in most subjects. You are welcome!

Timing the Exam

All examiners assume that you should read the paper first. It sounds like common sense. Reading the paper helps you familiarize yourself with it, so you get a sense of all the questions, and all the text. It gives you confidence that you know what you have to do. **All** the revision guides tell you to do this too.

Let me list some reasons why this is a stupid idea:

- Working memory is the amount of new learning you can cope with at any one time. This is limited: "there is an underlying limit on a central component of working memory, typically 3 to 5 chunks in young adults". So, just reading the questions on the paper will take up all of your working memory, in other words, reading the texts of the exam will not help you – little of it will stick in your memory.
  http://www.psychologicalscience.org/journals/cd/19_1_inpress/Cowan_final.pdf?q=the-recall-of-information-from-working-memory

- Many students read slowly, at least compared to the speed necessary in the exam. All the time you spend reading is time that you are not writing. It is **only** your writing that will score you any marks. So not writing = failing.

- The exam is the same for every student, even those who are not academic, but still need to score some marks. This means the examiners make sure easy marks are available at the beginning of each question. You need to start the questions straight away, so that you start earning the easy marks, and then have time for the difficult marks.

- If you are a really quick reader, what you are probably skilled at is not reading. Chances are you are skimming the text. But it should take you no more than three minutes, not 15.

- Lots of marks can be lost for making mistakes, any spare time in the exam is needed to check your answer, not for rereading the exam paper.

- If time ticks by while you are reading, you will actually lose confidence, knowing how little time is left.

- The grades for this exam are not only given to you because you have mastered certain skills. Instead, for candidates aiming at the old A and above, your exam level of 7, 8 and 9 is calculated by comparing your marks to the marks of everyone else in the country who sat the same exam. This means you need to start writing as soon as they do – and the best students will start writing almost straight away.

- Students used to be given two hours and 15 minutes for these papers. You now get 30 minutes less than students in previous years!

Your handwriting

Some of my students find it very unfair when I tell them that their handwriting will be judged. "But I've got messy handwriting sir, the content of what I've written is fine." True, but handwriting is a form of communication. If you can't "communicate with impact" then you can't get level 8. End of.

Examiners are usually teachers, and they want to give you the benefit of the doubt. But, if you don't close your vowels off, so your 'a's and 'o's look like 'u's, much of what you write won't make sense. If your 'm's look like 'w's, or 'n's, the same applies. If you don't leave a space between words, so the examiner can see where one ends and the other begins, the same applies. They will hate you just a little bit.

Here's another thing. The examiner is not paid by the hour. She is paid by the script (one student's answer). If she has to spend too long re-reading your script to work out what it says, she will lose patience, because she is losing money – the more scripts she gets through, the more she gets paid. So don't annoy the examiner. Really, I mean it.

You might think that it is inappropriate for me to write this way. It may well be, but I am trying to communicate to you the extreme annoyance your handwriting will provoke in the examiner.

And handwriting isn't just about this exam. It is about every exam, in every subject! How will you be able to read your own notes for A levels, from your lectures at university? What will happen when you sit your third year finals? How will an employer judge you if they can't read your handwriting?

Well, the obvious thing to do is to improve your handwriting.

You need to write quickly in the exam, so it needs to be cursive (joined up). This also has the added benefit of convincing the examiner that you are academic. **Academic writers don't print!**

An even better reason, is that joined up handwriting frees up space for thinking about what you are writing – the brain only has to focus on one word at a time. If you print, your brain is thinking about each letter at a time, so you have less capacity to think about the exam. This has a name, **cognitive load**, and it simply means that the more your brain has to think about, the less accurate it will be.

If you want to see how cognitive load works, start walking, and then think of a complicated sum, like 137 x 215. You will definitely slow your walk, and probably even stop. This is because the brain is overloaded even by walking at normal speed and thinking hard. Go on, try it.

Finally, cursive handwriting means that your brain remembers the shape of the whole word before you write it. This dramatically reduces the chance of making a spelling mistake. Most of my students believe that printing is neater than joined up handwriting. Usually this is wrong. It might look prettier, but it is often harder to read, because the spacing between letters and words is inconsistent. It only looks neater till you start to read it.

And this is another thing – academic people often do not have neat handwriting. But they have handwriting you can still read, even if it looks scruffy because they are writing so quickly. To get this standard of handwriting, you may have to start writing slowly. You won't be used to it. Practise in all your lessons, of whatever subject. This will help you to speed up gradually. Then try to keep it up for longer and longer.

Sometimes this still won't work (for example you might be reading this advice in April, with the exams just around the corner). In these circumstances, practice writing the first quarter of each answer in neat, cursive handwriting. Then speed up. The examiner will give you the benefit of the doubt here. She will see that you do write academically, use an excellent vocabulary and know exactly how to start your answer. When it comes to trying to decipher some messy handwriting later in the question, she is much more likely to assume it shares the same quality.

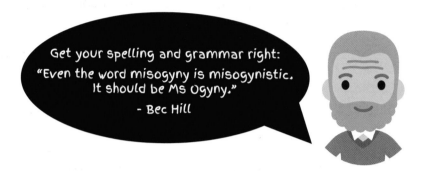

Get your spelling and grammar right:
"Even the word misogyny is misogynistic. It should be Ms Ogyny."
- Bec Hill

Your spelling and grammar

Questions 1 – 4 don't assess spelling, so in theory, it doesn't matter if your spelling is poor. But it does matter. Poor spelling is another way you will simply annoy the examiner. Really, I mean it. Your examiner is passionate about English. He reads books every day, for pleasure. He gets very annoyed when people say "less" instead of "fewer". He wants to slap someone who says "infers" when they mean "implies". When you choose to spell "soldier" as "solider" he counts to ten. When you spell "their" as "there" he curses you a little. When you write "weather" instead of "whether" or spell "disappear" as "dissapear" he takes you for a fool.

It doesn't matter that you have done most of what the question has asked, and got it right. As soon as there is any room for interpretation (and there is always room for interpretation) he won't give you the benefit of the doubt. The examiner will operate on a gut instinct, even though he is supposed to be objective. Being objective just isn't possible. You have offended him, devaluing things he cares about. He cannot think well of you, and above all, he cannot see you as academic. So, he will give you a lower mark.

Exam boards grade their examiners according to how accurate they are, A, B, C and D. If they are graded A, B and C, they get to carry on marking. Just think about what that means. It means that the examiner can be pretty inaccurate, only rated a B or C grade performer, **and their marks will still stand. So get the examiner on side**.

This is what Dr Chris Wheadon says about the exam regulator, Ofqual:
"The marking of English Language is likely to be extremely challenging this year. English Language has long answer questions, typically with 8, 16 and 24 mark responses. Ofqual's research suggests the following range of precision is normal across GCSE and A level:

- 8 mark items: +/- 3 marks
- 16 mark items: +/- 4 marks
- 24 mark items: +/- 6 marks

So, when an eight-mark item is marked, for the same response, it is normal for one marker to give four marks, while another will give seven marks. So, referring to the AQA mark scheme for English Language, one marker will mark a response as a 'Perceptive Summary' (Level 4) while another will mark it as 'Some attempts at summary' (Level 2). **Ofqual's research shows that this difference in opinion is a normal occurrence in marking of eight mark items**.

When a 16-mark item is marked, it is normal for one marker to give 12 marks, while another will give 16 marks, the difference between 'clear, relevant' and 'some attempts'.
When a 24-mark item is marked it is normal for one marker to give nine marks, and another to give 15 marks, which is the difference between 'simple, limited' and 'some success'.

To be clear, Ofqual's research is based on the differences that are normal for established specifications, after marker standardisation, and with the use by exam boards of sophisticated statistical rules which stop poor marking as soon as it is detected."

http://www.learningspy.co.uk/assessment/making-mockery-marking-new-gcse-english-language-mocks/

What does this mean?
It means that 50% of your marks are available for exam technique, for getting into the examiner's head. That's why this guide works so hard to give you 100%.

At the back of this guide is a list of the high frequency words you will need to use in the exam. Learn these spellings now, so that you will sound like an expert, so that your writing will be suitably academic.

Chapter 3: Paper 1, Question 1

Timing of questions

These are the marks for the questions:

Question 1	4 marks	6 minutes
Question 2	8 marks	12 minutes
Question 3	8 marks	12 minutes
Question 4	20 marks	30 minutes
Question 5	40 marks	45 minutes

The whole exam has a time limit of 1 hour and 45 minutes, or 105 minutes in total. The examiners advise you to spend 15 minutes reading, because they have not actually sat the exam. I have, and it's nonsense advice. It gives you too little time to get 100%. Instead, you need to answer each question as you read.

This means that, for the reading questions (which will always be questions 1, 2, 3 and 4), you will have 60 minutes to gain 40 marks. That means each mark should take you a minute and a half. This is how I have worked out your time limits above.

Question 1

Just tell me what to do
- Do this question last in section A, not first.
- Highlight the key words in the question which tell you what to look for
- Highlight the part of the text you are told to look at
- Look for four relevant facts
- Write each fact as a sentence
- If you can, quote within your sentence
- Give yourself six minutes to answer it

What does a question look like?
"Read again the first part of the source, lines 1 to 5. List four things from the start of the source about Goldilocks." [4 marks]

What does the mark scheme say?
- You must take your evidence from the part of the text the question tells you to look at
- You can quote or paraphrase
- A paraphrased response covering more than one point should be credited for each point made

What does the examiner really want?
- Four sentences
- Preferably with a quotation embedded in each

What do I have to do to get 100%?

(You are going to spend a maximum of six minutes on this question)

This question simply asks you to find four pieces of information in a text. The good news is that it does not matter whether or not you quote these facts. However, a quotation will always be a correct fact, which you can easily make into a sentence. So, if it looks easy to quote, then quote it.

The information should be easy to find, because even students at grade E and D, or 3 and 4, should be able to find it. Although it is likely that the information can be found easily, you may still have to read the whole text in order to answer. If you are not a fast reader, this is a slow way to get marks.

However, if you answer the longer questions first, you will have time to read the whole text. Furthermore, you will become completely familiar with the text. For this reason, it will probably be best to answer this question, question 1, last. You will find it much easier to find the answers.

There is another advantage. The first marks are always the easiest to get. Consequently, if you are running out of time on question 4, and you think you have only got 15 marks out of 20, you should simply stop it and do question 1. Why? Because getting four marks on question 1 will take you only about four minutes, because you know the text well by now. But getting the extra 4 marks, to score 19/20 on question 4, might take you 10 or 20 minutes, and that is time you just don't have.

Remember, the marks at the end of the question are always much, much harder to get. So, you should never go over time on a question. That same time, spent at the beginning of a question, will always earn you more marks.

Ok, so you're sitting in your mock, and you are going to answer it fourth. What can still go wrong?

"I wanted to do a show about feminism. But my husband wouldn't let me."
- Ria Lina

What are the common problems?

- Problem 1: Missing the right section of the text

The exam will probably ask you to find information from a section of the text (although it might make you read the whole text). For example, "Read again the first part of the source, lines 5 to 10. List four things from the start of the source about Goldilocks."

Well, the obvious problem is that there will be many facts about Goldilocks, all over the text. You might well choose facts from the wrong part. Even more likely, lines 1 to 4 are "the first part of the source". You might find that the first paragraph is lines 1 to 10, and so you will find evidence from the "first part", but it won't count because it is in lines 1 to 4 and not 5 to 10.

The examiners are not trying to catch you out here, but when I marked the mock papers in my school about 15% of students made this mistake, even those predicted grades 7, 8 and 9.

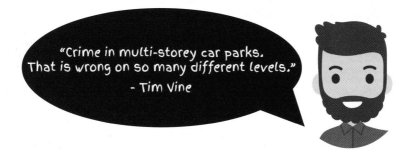

"Crime in multi-storey car parks. That is wrong on so many different levels."
- Tim Vine

- Problem 2: The wording of the question is designed to trick you

Part of the problem is the way the question is written. Imagine it was written like this:

"Read lines 1 to 5. From these lines, list four facts about Goldilocks."
This would make it much less likely that students would find facts from the wrong part of the text. So be prepared.

A sensible solution is to bring a highlighter to the exam. Highlight the key words in the question. These are the words that tell you where to look and what to write.

Read again the first part of the source, lines 5 to 10. List four things from the start of the source about Goldilocks."

Then go to the text, and highlight the relevant lines, by simply highlighting a line down the margin, next to the specific lines. This takes seconds, but makes sure that you answer the actual exam question, rather than, under exam pressure, what you think the question is.

- Problem 3: What is a list?

The next problem is the word "list". What does this mean? It will probably mean different things to different people, and this is a problem. What if your list is too brief for the examiner? A big clue is the fact that there will be two lines to write on for each of your four facts.

Many students will still write something like "blonde hair", rather than, "she wore long, blonde hair, arranged in a tangle of ringlets". While both of these count as a fact, the second one will definitely score the mark. The first one also might, depending on the key words in the mark scheme. But you don't want to risk that – it takes no time to write the extra. You will also note that the second one is also a sentence. The problem of writing a list which is too brief, and so fails to earn full marks happens to at least 25% of students in the mocks I've marked. So, write in sentences.

The good news is that there will probably be about six facts that you could find, not just four. If you find that you have only three, you might decide that one of your facts can be split. For example, my sentence above can become:

- She "wore long, blonde hair."
- Her hair was "arranged in a tangle of ringlets."

Again, I only do this if I can't find four facts.
I don't earn any extra marks for my quotation marks here, by the way. I can simply write without them:

- She wore long, blonde hair.
- Her hair was arranged in a tangle of ringlets.

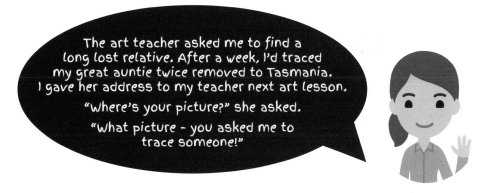

- Problem 4: Understanding long, complex sentences

The fourth problem is one of not reading carefully enough. The examiners may well try to catch you out here – they are trying to see if you can read for the right information after all. The confusion you experience as a reader will usually happen in a long, complex sentence.
Let's imagine this sentence in your "source":

"Goldilocks spooned her porridge with one hand, and with the other stroked the hair of the stuffed dog, smoking next to her, being too close to the fire."

Many students will read this in a hurry. They might decide that Goldilocks had a pet dog. Or that she was stroking her own hair. Or that she was smoking. Or that the dog was smoking a cigarette. Again, this is a very common kind of mistake, and will affect about 20% of mock answers I read.

This is another very good reason to do question 1 in fourth place. By this time, you will know the passage really well, and you will know that, for some reason, the bears have stuffed their dead dog, and Goldilocks has moved it too close to the fire, so that it is starting to catch alight.

Assessment objectives

The mark scheme, which you should read, always gives the assessment objectives of the question. You can find the mark scheme at: http://filestore.aqa.org.uk/resources/english/AQA-87001-SMS.PDF
Question 1 will always test this:

AO1:
- **Identify and interpret explicit and implicit information** and ideas
- Select and synthesise evidence from different texts.

However, the sample paper only focuses on the easy part of the skills, which I have highlighted in bold. It completely ignores point 2. This is because to "synthesise" is a higher level skill, and question

1 is aimed at any student who will get the equivalent of an E or a D. The ability to synthesise is instead tested in paper 2.

But the key to the first point, even when you are aiming for the top grades, is that when you "identify" a fact it is quite possible that you will "interpret" incorrectly. If the examiner wants to catch you out, they will find an extract that needs a little interpretation, as we saw with Goldilocks and the stuffed dog.
Model answer:
Goldilocks ate "the large bowl of porridge" first.
Goldilocks thought the second bowl of porridge "was too cold".
Goldilocks broke the chair that was "just right" by sitting in it.
Goldilocks slept in the "baby bear's bed".

(Notice that, where possible, I have included embedded quotations).

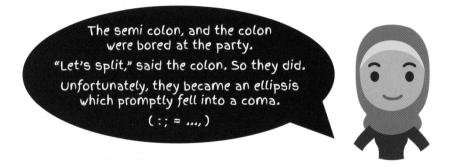

Chapter 4: Paper 1, Question 2

Question 2 is always a question about language.
This means you must always quote.

Just tell me what to do

- Highlight the key words in the question which tell you what to look for
- Highlight the margin of the part of the text you are told to look at
- Find quotations as you read
- Name a descriptive or narrative technique for each quotation you use
  (These will always be about imagery – simile, metaphor, personification, alliteration – and then perhaps onomatopoeia, sibilance, synesthesia, assonance, pathetic fallacy)
- Refer to individual words in the quotation
- Name their parts of speech – verb, adverb, noun, adjective
- Find a long complex sentence, especially one with listed descriptions
- Comment on the effect of contrast or juxtaposition, which will be in any description
- Relate these quotations to the writer's purpose, to discuss their effects
- Use tentative language, like 'perhaps' to suggest your interpretation of the effect or purpose
- Do not write in PEE paragraphs, but sentences which include embedded quotations

What does the question look like?

Here is a typical question:

Look in detail at this extract from lines **5 to 12** of the source:
(Extract in question paper)

How does the writer use language here to describe The Big Bad Wolf? You could include the writer's choice of:

- words and phrases
- language features and techniques
- sentence forms.

(The highlighted words will stay the same in every question 2)

What does the mark scheme say?

You will:
- Have detailed and perceptive understanding of language
- Analyse the effects of the writer's choices of language

- Use a range of quotations, and choose them well
- Use a wide range of subject terminology accurately

What does the examiner really want?

Ok, let's get busy with the highlighter again. What are the words which tell you where to look and what to write?

Look in detail at this extract from lines 5 to 12 of the source:
(Extract in question paper)

How does the writer use language here to describe The Big Bad Wolf? You could include the writer's choice of:
- words and phrases
- language features and techniques
- sentence forms.

This question is interesting. My highlighting show me that I need to write about The Big Bad Wolf and not Grandma or Little Red Riding Hood. The question will always ask you to look at some description. Because it is a language question, the examiner wants you to quote.

The problem students have is with "sentence forms". My advice to you is always to write about complex sentences or, if your extract doesn't have any, write about why not. Because you want 100%, I'm going to set out below why I recommend you should do this, as well as how to do it.

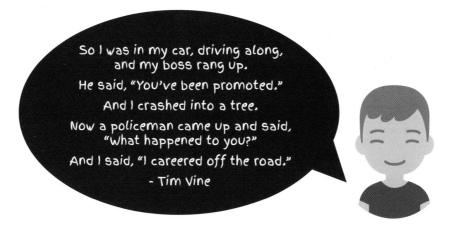

So I was in my car, driving along,
and my boss rang up.
He said, "You've been promoted."
And I crashed into a tree.
Now a policeman came up and said,
"What happened to you?"
And I said, "I careered off the road."
- Tim Vine

Why should you write about complex sentences?

Ok, as an English Language and Literature graduate, I never once had to write about an author's use of complex sentences – it is not something that experts in English care about. So, this skill is just for the exam – it is artificial, not real English, but I am going to show you how to do it properly.

The English teachers who wrote the exam probably agree with me – writing about complex, compound, and simple sentences doesn't have much to do with English. That is why the word "could" appears in question 2. You "could" write about "sentence forms", but equally you "could" write about other language features.

So, at its most basic, this question asks you to be able to quote, and use the correct terminology when you write about the effect of the language. I'll show you what that looks like in a minute.

However, this is a new exam. It is very likely that the examiner who wrote the question paper and the mark scheme is a different person from the examiner who wrote the exemplar of a model answer, which also appears in the mark scheme. For example, the top answer for the specimen paper on *Brighton Rock* (your teacher can get this from eAQA for free), might contain something like this, which is written as the exemplar in the mark scheme:

> The long detailed complex sentence perhaps suggests the movement of the many tourists on their tram trip into town.

So, although you "could" decide not to write about complex sentences, the exemplar deliberately puts one in. This will confuse many examiners, who will therefore interpret the mark scheme differently. The use of "perhaps" also shows how even the examiners are not sure if this is what the complex sentence shows. Consequently, **you must write about complex sentences**, so there can be no element of doubt in the examiner's mind when they ask, "does this student do what is in the mark scheme?" I will show you how to do this better than the examiners!

Your teacher might tell you that you don't need to write about complex sentences. I hope you can see why they would do this and still be factually correct, and also why I think you should do it anyway.

Teachers in my school have attended meetings with AQA, where they are told that students do not need to write about complex and simple sentence types. Instead, they should write about the use of statements, or dialogue, or rhetorical questions. However, most description will not have any of these sentence forms, so this advice is not helpful. On the other hand, I will try to show you that just about any description the exam will give you will have complex sentences, about which you can write.

What do I have to do to get 100%?

How to write about complex sentences in question 2

Let's look again at my paraphrasing of the examiner's exemplar:

> The long detailed complex sentence perhaps suggests the movement of the many tourists on their tram trip into town.

I can't quote the extract from Graham Greene's *Brighton Rock* for copyright reasons. It can be found by your teacher at eAQA.

When you read it, you will see that Graham Greene does not want to focus on the movement of the crowd at all. To show you what I mean, I'll use what Greene wrote, but in a very interesting way.

Think like a writer
To understand how complex sentences might help a writer, you have to think like a writer. So, I am going to do something that you should try yourself. I am going to write a similar paragraph to the one in the sample paper, using the same punctuation, a similar number of verbs and noun phrases, and of course the same descriptive techniques. To keep the examiner's comment relevant, I'll include a tram as Greene did, even though Paris (where I am setting it) has a metro instead.

My version of Brighton Rock
They flooded into Paris from St Pancras every hour, stumbled down the Champs Elysees crowding the tops of trams, dismounted in lemming-like crowds into the clamour of angry traffic: the tricoleur danced on the streetlamps, the ornate buildings stood grandly in ranks like a Napoleonic regiment: a

conman demonstrating 'hunt the lady', buskers playing, man-made beaches by the river, and billboards desperate to capture your wallet in vibrant colours clashing across the city's walls.

It seemed quite easy to Mr. Salles to be lost in Paris.

What to notice in the complex sentences in this text
Here, you can see I am not interested in any way in onward movement. I am much more interested, as Graham Greene is, in the spectacle of the city, perhaps its chaos, certainly its vibrant nature, perhaps an element of threat in the foreign environment. It is totally irrelevant that this is a complex sentence, and much more relevant that it is a list.

However, in my answer, I will use the words "complex sentence" because, as we have seen, the examiners seem to be pointing us this way. I'm also going to use it because, in virtually any piece of description you are likely to meet in the exam, you will meet a complex sentence. But the point I make about it will be about the structure of the sentence. In this case it is a list – so I will write about the point of this particular list. If I'm really good, I'll try to write about more than one purpose to the list. This is what will get the marks. This is what will tell the examiner that my answer is "sophisticated".

"The long complex sentence works as a detailed list of sights that reflect the spectacle of the city and how the travelers can get lost in its many attractions and **perhaps** its hidden dangers."

I hope you can see the three purposes to the list I have highlighted here:

"The long complex sentence works as a detailed list of sights that reflect the spectacle of the city and how the travelers can get lost in its many attractions and perhaps its hidden dangers."

Using "perhaps" is very useful. It tells me that in my next paragraph I need to write about the suggestion of danger, suggested by the "conman", the "angry traffic", the buildings in "ranks" like an army, and the threat to the travelers' budgets from the advertising and pressure to buy. In this way, my "perhaps" forces me to be sophisticated, because it will force me to think about other interpretations, contrasting the positive and the negative.

So, you will also use a 'perhaps' to explain why the complex sentence is used.

Complex sentences and contrast or juxtaposition

Nearly all description works this way. Good writers are always playing with our expectations, making us work hard to predict which way they are going to jump – positive or negative. This gives their writing an element of conflict. Conflict is what all novels are about. And contrast is the easiest way to push the narrative towards conflict.

Another point which I should emphasise is that I don't need a degree to learn this. I learn this by imitation. Through copying *Brighton Rock*, in as close detail as I can manage, I learn to think like a writer. If you want to be brilliant at English, I can't recommend this technique enough. It will prepare you perfectly for the exam, but it will also make you a brilliant writer, and that is a skill which will last for life.

Trust me – I'm a writer!

I started to write with a broken pencil, but it was pointless.

Summary

So, to summarise the key points about complex sentences so far:

- You will always mention a complex sentence – if there is one, and there is almost definitely one in any piece of description.
- You will write about why this level of detail is there (you will probably nearly always be able to refer to it as a list, because descriptions work that way).
- Even if it is not a list, you will write about why that level of detail is there.
- You'll use "perhaps" to introduce more than one purpose.
- Write about contrast, or the senses.

Chapter 5: Does Description Usually Involve Complex Sentences and a List?

Read this section if you want to see how complex sentences work in descriptive writing.

Does all description work this way with complex sentences? Let's put "Dickens' description of London" into Google, to see what extracts other writers choose from Dickens:

Little Dorrit

In *Little Dorrit*, Dickens describes a London rainstorm:

"In the country, the rain would have developed a thousand fresh scents, and every drop would have had its bright association with some beautiful form of growth or life. In the city, it developed only foul stale smells, and was a sickly, lukewarm, dirt- stained, wretched addition to the gutters."

Explanation of the effect of the complex sentences
Here both lists are used to develop a contrast, the purpose of which is to show how unappealing London is compared to nature.

All the toilets in London police stations have been stolen.
Police say they have nothing to go on.

Household Words
In an article for *Household Words* in March 1851 Dickens, with characteristic sarcasm, describes the environmental impact of having live cattle markets and slaughterhouses in the city:

"In half a quarter of a mile's length of Whitechapel, at one time, there shall be six hundred newly slaughtered oxen hanging up, and seven hundred sheep but, the more the merrier proof of prosperity. Hard by Snow Hill and Warwick Lane, you shall see the little children, inured to sights of brutality from their birth, trotting along the alleys, mingled with troops of horribly busy pigs, up to their ankles in blood but it makes the young rascals hardy. Into the imperfect sewers of this overgrown city, you shall have the immense mass of corruption, engendered by these practices, lazily thrown out of sight, to rise, in poisonous gases, into your house at night, when your sleeping children will most readily absorb them, and to find its languid way, at last, into the river that you drink."

Explanation of the effect of the complex sentences

Here again the complex sentences are a list of the full horrors of London, immersing us in all of these through the use of all the senses. Again, contrast is used to show the damaging effect London has on the once innocent children.

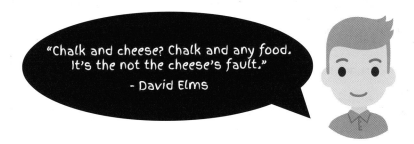

"Chalk and cheese? Chalk and any food.
It's the not the cheese's fault."
- David Elms

Oliver Twist

In *Oliver Twist*, Dickens describes the scene as Oliver and Bill Sikes travel through the Smithfield live-cattle market on their way to burglarize the Maylie home:

"It was market-morning. The ground was covered, nearly ankle-deep, with filth and mire; a thick steam, perpetually rising from the reeking bodies of the cattle, and mingling with the fog, which seemed to rest upon the chimney-tops, hung heavily above. All the pens in the centre of the large area, and as many temporary pens as could be crowded into the vacant space, were filled with sheep; tied up to posts by the gutter side were long lines of beasts and oxen, three or four deep. Countrymen, butchers, drovers, hawkers, boys, thieves, idlers, and vagabonds of every low grade, were mingled together in a mass; the whistling of drovers, the barking dogs, the bellowing and plunging of the oxen, the bleating of sheep, the grunting and squeaking of pigs, the cries of hawkers, the shouts, oaths, and quarrelling on all sides; the ringing of bells and roar of voices, that issued from every public-house; the crowding, pushing, driving, beating, whooping and yelling; the hideous and discordant dim that resounded from every corner of the market; and the unwashed, unshaven, squalid, and dirty figures constantly running to and fro, and bursting in and out of the throng; rendered it a stunning and bewildering scene, which quite confounded the senses."

Explanation of the effect of the complex sentences

Here Dickens is up to exactly the same tricks with his complex sentence – this one has become a masterclass of how to extend the list. The purpose of this one is to emphasise the great clamour of noises in the London market.

I'm not developing these points, I am just giving you a quick glimpse to see whether my instincts are right: all description is likely to rely on complex sentences, and these will very often be in the form of a list. We will always be able to write about a purpose of the list. This will usually be connected to the idea of contrast, or to the senses, or both.

Look for characters at http://charlesdickenspage.com/reading_dickens.html

Ok, let's now look at a different writer. Let's try Conrad, and the first extract I find from *Heart of Darkness*:

"A slight clinking behind me made me turn my head. Six black men advanced in a file, toiling up the path. They walked erect and slow, balancing small baskets full of earth on their heads, and the clink kept time with their footsteps. Black rags were wound round their loins, and the short ends behind waggled to and fro like tails. I could see every rib, the joints of their limbs were like knots in a rope;

each had an iron collar on his neck, and all were connected together with a chain whose bights swung between them, rhythmically clinking."

So, here again we have the long, complex sentence, in a list. Here, we suspect the writer is horrified at the treatment of the black men. Again, Conrad uses the senses, especially sound, to emphasise the presence of the metal chains that enslave the men.

The extract continues:
"Another report from the cliff made me think suddenly of that ship of war I had seen firing into a continent. It was the same kind of ominous voice; but these men could by no stretch of imagination be called enemies. They were called criminals, and the outraged law, like the bursting shells, had come to them, an insoluble mystery from the sea. All their meagre breasts panted together, the violently dilated nostrils quivered, the eyes stared stonily uphill. They passed me within six inches, without a glance, with that complete, deathlike indifference of unhappy savages. Behind this raw matter one of the reclaimed, the product of the new forces at work, strolled despondently, carrying a rifle by its middle. He had a uniform jacket with one button off, and seeing a white man on the path, hoisted his weapon to his shoulder with alacrity. This was simple prudence, white men being so much alike at a distance that he could not tell who I might be. He was speedily reassured, and with a large, white, rascally grin, and a glance at his charge, seemed to take me into partnership in his exalted trust. After all, I also was a part of the great cause of these high and just proceedings."

Here is an extract from the first chapter of *Kim*, by Rudyard Kipling, describing him as a young boy.

"As he reached the years of indiscretion, he learned to avoid missionaries and white men of serious aspect who asked who he was, and what he did. For Kim did nothing with an immense success. True, he knew the wonderful walled city of Lahore from the Delhi Gate to the outer Fort Ditch; was hand in glove with men who led lives stranger than anything Haroun al Raschid dreamed of; and he lived in a life wild as that of the Arabian Nights, but missionaries and secretaries of charitable societies could not see the beauty of it. His nickname through the wards was 'Little Friend of all the World'; and very often, being lithe and inconspicuous, he executed commissions by night on the crowded housetops for sleek and shiny young men of fashion. It was intrigue, - of course he knew that much, as he had known all evil since he could speak, - but what he loved was the game for its own sake - the stealthy prowl through the dark gullies and lanes, the crawl up a water pipe, the sights and sounds of the women's world on the flat roofs, and the headlong flight from housetop to housetop under cover of the hot dark."

Have a play with some of these extracts and see if you can come up with reasons for particular complex sentences.

If you post your writing on my YouTube channel, Mr. Salles Teaches English, I will reply to you, or better still, make a video out of it. Try your own versions of questions 2, 3 or 4. Or, if you are interested in become great at English, imitate an extract, as I did with *Brighton Rock*, and post it on my channel also.

Q: What's black and white, and red all over?
A: A newspaper?
A: No, badger road-kill.

Model answer

Look in detail at this extract **from** lines 1 to 9 of the source:
(Extract in question paper)

How does the writer use language to describe Paris? You could include the writer's choice of:
- Words and phrases
- Language features and techniques
- Sentence forms

They flooded into Paris from St Pancras every hour, stumbled down the Champs Elysees crowding the tops of trams, dismounted in lemming-like crowds into the clamour of angry traffic: the tricoleur danced on the streetlamps, the ornate buildings stood grandly in ranks like a Napoleonic regiment: a conman demonstrating 'hunt the lady', buskers playing, man-made beaches by the river, and billboards desperate to capture your wallet in vibrant colours clashing across the city's walls.

It seemed quite easy to Mr. Salles to be lost in Paris. Two hundred thousand tourists as well as himself were here today, and for several hours, Mr. Salles surrendered to pleasure, drinking champagne whenever his sightseeing allowed.

The extract section will be around 110-130 words, so one skill you must develop is that of finding techniques quickly.

At all times, you need to name the techniques. You will get marked down if you name them wrongly. The next skill is being able to explain "the writer's use", which means the same as explaining the effect on the reader. This is because that is the only reason the writer is using any language, to control the thoughts and feelings of their readers.

In my determination to get 100%, I'm going to practice writing my answer under exam conditions, and I'm going to do it without stopping. You will see this in my video at: https://www.youtube.com/watch?v=xJpLA81fKLo

But, because you are learning, you need to keep a record of how many words you wrote, how many points you made, and what mark you got. Then, the next time you attempt a question 2, you'll look at the same three totals, to see how you are improving. Put simply, the more techniques you can write about in the time available, the higher your grade will be.

Just as the examiner does in the exemplar, I am going to make sure that my first point is about the complex sentence.

And obviously I am going to spend exactly 12 minutes on it.

Model 12-minute answer

The main technique Mr. Salles uses is contrast. The long, detailed complex sentence at the beginning serves to create a vibrant description of Paris. However, the complexity is added to by the contrast between the positive and the negative. So, Paris is full of spectacle, "ornate buildings", "vibrant colours", which are juxtaposed with more threatening images: the buildings are arranged in "ranks" like an army and the streets are filled with threatening, personified "angry traffic".

Paris is filled with "lemming-like crowds", as though the tourists are so stupid that they become victims of the city. This means that they are likely to fall prey to the "conman" or advertising, suggested by the personification of the "desperate" billboards. However, this is contrasted to Mr. Salles, who sees Paris as a place of "pleasure". The threats that are perceived in the first paragraph are contrasted with his reaction, so that he "surrendered to pleasure". This picks up on the earlier threat of Paris described as a dangerous army, where its buildings were personified as "like a Napoleonic regiment", but transforms it. Mr. Salles appears to have decided Paris is so wonderful, it is best to surrender to it, rather than fight the attraction.

Another contrast is the suggestion that the tourists might be just as threatening to Paris. Perhaps the traffic is "angry" in response to the "lemming-like" behaviour of the crowds. Similarly, the use of the verb "flooded" to describe the tourists' arrival also suggests that they are damaging to the city. Possibly they outnumber the locals, like a flood washes away what was there. Or perhaps they are washing away an atmosphere that the Parisians might otherwise enjoy: the "ornate buildings", the "champagne" or the patriotism and pride symbolized by the "tricoleur", without the invasion of foreign tourists.

The overall effect is to introduce an element of conflict, which encourages us to speculate as to how it will be resolved for Mr. Salles.

[322 words in 12 minutes.]

In highlighting is my use of subject terminology.
Here are some of the things I'd like you to learn from my answer:

- Start with the **main technique**. I chose contrast. I predict that most descriptions use contrast because, as I have said, they introduce conflict, and conflict is what drives the plot of all novels. So:

- You will probably be able to begin with the idea of **contrast or conflict**.

- Stating that it is the main technique tells your examiner that you have read the whole passage, found lots of techniques in it, and evaluated which one you think is most important. This is a perfect way to get inside the examiner's head, and get them to see you as an expert.

- The next point I make is deliberately linked to "**sentence forms**" as I want to make sure that I get every bullet point in. This is the one that I am most likely to forget, and more importantly, that most students are likely to do badly. To control the examiner's thoughts, I put this in first so that she will see me as an expert.

- I use the shortest quotations that I can, because I can make more points about language this way. It also has a name, **embedding quotations**, and this is a skill that will make me write like an expert. My quotations fit into my sentences. This means that my explanation for the quotation happens in the same sentence, meaning my writing is much more fluent – I say more with fewer words. This is crucial, because I have only 12 minutes to write. Don't waste words.

- The exam criteria will always have the word "sophisticated" in it. But the examiner won't explain what this means. How do you learn to be sophisticated? Writing about reading always involves looking at more than one interpretation. I can force myself to always **write about alternative interpretations** by using these words: **"contrast", "however", "juxtapose"**.

- Another way to be sophisticated is to explore your original idea in more depth. Instead of just writing more about the quotation, I would teach you instead to use these words: **"possibly", "perhaps"**. This tentative language forces you to consider ideas, and forces you to be sophisticated. It means you won't add extra detail that is simply waffle.

- It may seem obvious, but I **paragraph**. Again, about 25% of mock answers I mark have no paragraphs in them, because the students just forget in the heat of the exam. If you don't paragraph, the examiner will think you are stupid, and mark you down, regardless of the quality of your ideas.

- I don't write a conclusion that begins with "in conclusion". Instead I write about the overall effect, and I make sure that this is just one sentence long.

- I **highlighted my key words in the question**. This was really important at the end, when I actually wanted to write about Mr. Salles, because that is what the paragraph was about. However, that wouldn't answer the question, which is about Paris. So, this reminded me to relate what I said about Mr. Salles to Paris.

- Every time I have written about a literary technique, I have named it. I've also used the language of the expert to describe features of the writing.

- I have used the word **"suggests" instead of shows**, as that is more formal. **"Implies" and "indicates"** would work just as well.

- I have never used the word "also", because it doesn't sound like the language of an expert.

- In my answer, I try never to write a simple sentence, unless it is the topic sentence of each paragraph (the topic sentence is the first sentence, and gives a clear idea to the examiner about what the whole paragraph will discuss). **Nearly every other sentence is complex, with at least one comma in it**. The reasons for that are that this is the way experts write. They do this for the added benefit of making sure each sentence has more than one idea in it. This therefore leads to your getting more marks).

- I've also **never used the word "quotation"**, because the quotation marks already tell the reader that it is a quotation – I don't have to tell them twice.

These are a lot of skills for you to master. Don't worry that you will never get there – you will. The first time you answer a question, it might be only five skills that you get. Then you might only master one or two more each time you attempt the question. However, these skills are relevant to questions 2, 3 and 4 on paper 1, and 2, 3, 4 on paper 2. So, if you just do one each of those questions for your revision, you are likely to go from being able to do five of the above to 12, even if you only improve by one skill at a time.

It's not a question of having the brains, it is simply a question of doing the work. Obviously, you will have some questions where you don't get better – you might get stuck on nine or ten of the above techniques for a while. But keep practising. After all, if you sit two papers as part of your revision, you will practice the skill 14 times instead of once. That will only take you about four hours, but will represent most of the skills of both reading papers. This guide will only help you if you do that – put into practice the techniques I am teaching you. Aim for 100%.

"My name is Fin, which means it's very hard for me to end emails without sounding pretentious."
- Fin Taylor

The mark scheme

I can get most of the marks without looking at the mark scheme, simply by writing as an expert. However, as we saw earlier, I would still fail to get full marks with some examiners, if I did not write about complex sentences. So, let's look at the mark scheme in a bit more detail:

- **Have detailed and perceptive understanding of language**

I have been **detailed**. I simply wrote for 12 minutes. I never ask, "how much should I write?" because that is irrelevant. For example, it is very likely that my first two paragraphs, at 201 words, would be "detailed" enough to get full marks. Would I stop there? No, because I have not used up my 12 minutes.

Similarly, I might only have written 150 words at the end of 12 minutes. Would I carry on to 200 because Mr. Salles's guide said that was how much to write? No, because that would take time away from another question. And the first few marks on the next question are always easier to get than the last marks on any question.

Finally, because the mark scheme does not say how much is detailed, there is no reliable guide – each examiner will have a different idea. So, write as much as you can in the time limit, and no more. I have been **perceptive**. Go back over my list of 1-14 above, and work out which ones tell the examiners you are perceptive.

- **Analyse the effects of the writer's choices of language**

I hope you haven't cheated. The only one that doesn't show you are **perceptive** was number 8.

How have I **analysed**? By using the techniques above in 3, 5, 6, 7, 11, 12, and 14. How have I written about the **effects of the writer's** language? By using the techniques in 1, 2, 5, 6, 7, 11, 12, 14.

- **Use a range of quotations, and choose them well**

Have I used a **range** of quotations? Yes, they come from all parts of the passage, and there is a quotation in nearly every sentence, apart from the topic sentence of each paragraph.

Has my range been **judicious** (which means well chosen)? How can an examiner tell? The technique that always makes the examiner think that you have is five. But in using embedded quotations, you will also inevitably use so many of the other techniques too – they all start from getting five right first.

- **Use a wide range of subject terminology accurately**

Has my use of terminology been **sophisticated**? Like **judicious**, this is a bit of a gut reaction criteria for the examiner. It really means, has the student got into your head and persuaded you they write like an expert. In other words, can they do most of 1 – 15 above?

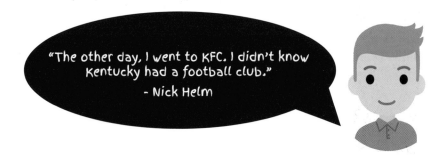

"The other day, I went to KFC. I didn't know Kentucky had a football club."
- Nick Helm

Chapter 6: The Problem with PEE Paragraphs

(And PEED, PEA, PEAL, PEEL etc.!)

The problem with PEE paragraphs is that they are a great way to first teach the structure of paragraphing when you need to use quotations to back up a point of view. But, PEE paragraphs (and their cousins, PEEE, PEED, PEA, PEAL and PEEL) are really no more than stabilizers on a bicycle. Yes, they'll steer you to riding the bike, but they won't teach you to balance it like an expert. Similarly, to write like an expert, like an academic or a scholar, you are going to need to move beyond PEE paragraphs.

Ok, now I'm going to give you the same answer, written in PEE paragraphs, to show you why you shouldn't use them.

Model answer as PEE paragraphs

Here is the second paragraph of my answer, re-written as PEE paragraphs:

Paris is filled with lots of people. This is shown by the quotation "lemming-like crowds". This suggests that the tourists are so stupid that they become victims of the city. They also become victims in other ways. For example, the quotation "conman" implies that Parisians try to take tourists' money. Another quotation is "billboards desperate to capture your wallet" which reinforces this. This is personification.

However, this is contrasted to Mr. Salles, who sees Paris as a place of "pleasure". This means he is not scared of the dangers of Paris. The threats that are perceived in the first paragraph are contrasted with his reaction. We can tell this from the quotation "surrendered to pleasure". This picks up on the earlier threat of Paris described as a dangerous army, where its buildings were personified. This is shown in the quotation "like a Napoleonic regiment", which is also a simile.

This is now 149 words long, where my version was only 104. That doesn't sound like much, but actually it means I have bought 30% more time in the exam **by not using PEE**. Imagine how many more marks you will get than the student who doesn't write like an expert!

Remember, I haven't changed any of the meaning of my paragraph to make it follow a PEE structure – both mean exactly the same. However, would one score higher marks? Probably. When you read the PEE paragraph version, it feels clunky. Writing PEE paragraphs has also forced me to start several sentences with 'this', so that I sound much less like an expert.

The reason for that is that the explanation is kept separate from the point and the evidence (quotation). In my paragraph, the point and explanation often appear in the same sentence. Because my quotations are embedded, they appear in the same sentence a lot of the time too. This simply makes the writing feel more fluent.

Summary

- Once you already know how to write in PEE paragraphs, get rid of them.
- Try to have at least two, and often three of your point, evidence, and explanation in the same sentence.
- Analyse language and the effect on the reader using 1 – 14 above.
- When you have done so, show your writing to your teacher, or post them on my channel.

A plateau is a high form of flattery.

Chapter 7: Paper 1, Question 3

Just tell me what to do

- Highlight the key words in the question which tell you what to look for
- Highlight in the margin of the part of the text you are told to look at
- Identify structural techniques as you read
    - Always write about **beginnings** and **endings**
    - Shifts of perspective or focus
    - Paragraphing and topic change
    - How sentences contribute to the whole text's structure
    - Contrast and juxtaposition (but see 4 below)
    - Repetition
    - The order in which information is revealed, or hidden
    - Clues about the context which may be important
    - How a climax is built up
    - How the reader is invited to make predictions – which may be deliberately misleading
- Don't repeat anything you wrote in question 2
- Relate all of these that you find to the effect on the reader

What does the question look like?

This question asks you to think about the structure of the whole text. This is the skill that teachers are likely to teach least well, because it is new to them. Previous GCSEs have never really focused on how texts are structured, so it may be that a lot of what I am teaching you here is different from what you have learned in class.

Assessment objective 2
AO2:
- Analyse how writers use language and structure
- To achieve effects and influence readers
- Using relevant subject terminology to support their views.

This question assesses how the writer has structured a text.
Structural features can be:

- Beginnings and endings
- Shifts of perspective or focus
- Paragraphing and topic change
- How sentences contribute to the whole text's structure.

"To the man on crutches, dressed in camouflage, who stole my wallet ... you can hide but you can't run."
- Milton Jones

Question 3

"You now need to think about the whole of the source. This text is from the opening of a short story.

How has the writer structured the text to interest you as a reader? You could write about:

- what the writer focuses your attention on at the beginning
- how and why the writer changes this focus as the source develops
- any other structural features that interest you."

[12 marks]

(The highlighted words are my key words, the ones that I will highlight in the exam, so I answer the entire question)

Again, like the word "could" in question 2, the word "can" means that any other aspects of structure you write about will also count.

The examiner's answer

To double check this, we need to look at the exemplar written by the examiner. The examiner bases her whole answer on the focus of the writing. First it is on the city, then on the main character Hale, then inside Hale's thoughts. The examiner also looks for contrast, in this case how the city and the crowd are deliberately contrasted to Hale. She makes a point of looking at the structure of the beginning and the ending – the contrast with the city occurring at the beginning, and the ending with its final focus on Hale.

Interestingly, it is only when dealing with the ending that the examiner discusses **the effect on the reader**. This is a high risk approach! I will teach you how to deal with the effect on the reader more frequently.

Ok, before I summarise what the mark scheme teaches us that we have to do, let's look at the instructions in the question:

As you can see, the examiner gives us a strong hint that we should write about the beginning of the text. The need to write about the ending is hidden, and not in the question. This means that, in the examiner's mind, writing about the ending is going to be a deciding factor in giving the higher grades. This point also fits with what we found earlier, where the examiner talked about the effect on the reader only when dealing with the ending – this is a powerful clue that writing about the ending of the text, and comparing it to other parts of the texts, is going to get you the highest marks.
Under exam pressure, you will probably just move through the passage chronologically, so if you run out of time, it is most likely that the part of the text you don't write about is the ending. Beware of this!

What does the mark scheme say?

Before you attempt to write your answer (yes, the best use of this guide is to write your answer, then look at mine later) let's look at the top criteria in the mark scheme.
You will:

- Be detailed
- Be perceptive
- Discuss structural features
- Analyse the effect on the reader
- Use a range of quotations from the whole of the text
- Use subject terminology frequently and accurately

You should notice that the skills are exactly the same as in question 2, except the word "language" has been changed to "structural". You should also notice that the examiner has placed "structural" in italics. This is because they know teachers are likely to focus too much on language, instead of structure. Even more importantly, this is also for examiners – AQA's senior examiners clearly worry that their own examiners won't focus enough on students' sticking to the "structure" of the text. This is very good news for you, because it means that a total focus on structure will gain you top marks.

Because I want to write about the author's tone – and I want you to write about it too – we need to be very careful to relate this precisely to the structure of the story.

"If I'm ever feeling down I just type: 'yo are the best,' into Google.

Then it responds: 'I think you mean: you are the best' and I feel much better."
- Jack Barry

Ok, but what does the examiner really want?

All the guides I have read suggest that you just write about the changes in focus. You can do this. But this is a very narrow view of structure. AQA's own textbook actually pretends that the extract is a film and uses phrases like close up, zooming in and wide angle. You can do this, but it shouldn't get you 100%.

Questions to ask about structure

- What effect does the beginning have on our expectations of what will happen later?
- How does the inclusion of this detail lead us to make a prediction?
- Why is this the first detail revealed about the character?
- What does the writer include to change our opinion of the character?
- Why is this the first point of the argument?
- Why does the writer overuse a particular word class - adjective, adverb, or sometimes verbs?
- What are the effects of writing such long, list-like sentences?
- How does the writer control the pace of the writing?
- What is the effect of the sound of these words: look at alliteration, onomatopoeia, sibilance?
- Why doesn't the writing end there, but instead here (look at a previous paragraph).

A sense of an ending

Because we are dealing with structure, it is possible that the examiners will choose to give you an ending, rather than a beginning. I feel this is unlikely, for several reasons. There are many more structural techniques in an opening – the writer needs to lay many more clues, fleshing out characters, hinting at or a developing a crisis, foreshadowing possible future events, which invite the reader to predict. An ending does few of those things, and perhaps none.

However, there are other features of endings that it is worth knowing. These will always be useful if a question on endings comes up in the exam, but they will also be useful in your writing about the structure of a crisis.

Another huge advantage, is that they will also be very relevant in writing about the literature texts you study. If you watch my *Of Mice and Men*, *The Strange Case of Dr Jekyll and Mr Hyde* or *An Inspector Calls* videos, you will know that I always tell my student to write about the ending of the text, as this is when the author's purpose and viewpoint is most clearly expressed.

So, let's look at the ending to A Christmas Carol. Again this is a 19th century text, with challenging language. Read it and decide what you think Dickens' purpose is. ("Intercourse" does not carry the modern meaning – remember how to decode words that your uncertain of).

Ending of *A Christmas Carol*, by Charles Dickens

But he was early at the office next morning. Oh, he was early there. If he could only be there first, and catch Bob Cratchit coming late! That was the thing he had set his heart upon.

And he did it; yes, he did! The clock struck nine. No Bob. A quarter past. No Bob. He was full eighteen minutes and a half behind his time. Scrooge sat with his door wide open, that he might see him come into the Tank.

His hat was off, before he opened the door; his comforter too. He was on his stool in a jiffy; driving away with his pen, as if he were trying to overtake nine o'clock.

"Hallo!" growled Scrooge, in his accustomed voice, as near as he could feign it. "What do you mean by coming here at this time of day?"

"I am very sorry, sir," said Bob. "I am behind my time."

"You are?" repeated Scrooge. "Yes. I think you are. Step this way, sir, if you please."

"It's only once a year, sir," pleaded Bob, appearing from the Tank. "It shall not be repeated. I was making rather merry yesterday, sir."

"Now, I'll tell you what, my friend," said Scrooge, "I am not going to stand this sort of thing any longer. And therefore," he continued, leaping from his stool, and giving Bob such a dig in the waistcoat that he staggered back into the Tank again; "and therefore I am about to raise your salary!"

Bob trembled, and got a little nearer to the ruler. He had a momentary idea of knocking Scrooge down with it, holding him, and calling to the people in the court for help and a strait-waistcoat.

"A merry Christmas, Bob!" said Scrooge, with an earnestness that could not be mistaken, as he clapped him on the back. "A merrier Christmas, Bob, my good fellow, than I have given you, for many a year!

I'll raise your salary, and endeavour to assist your struggling family, and we will discuss your affairs this very afternoon, over a Christmas bowl of smoking bishop, Bob! Make up the fires, and buy another coal-scuttle before you dot another i, Bob Cratchit!"

Scrooge was better than his word. He did it all, and infinitely more; and to Tiny Tim, who did not die, he was a second father. He became as good a friend, as good a master, and as good a man, as the good old city knew, or any other good old city, town, or borough, in the good old world. Some people laughed to see the alteration in him, but he let them laugh, and little heeded them; for he was wise enough to know that nothing ever happened on this globe, for good, at which some people did not have their fill of laughter in the outset; and knowing that such as these would be blind anyway, he thought it quite as well that they should wrinkle up their eyes in grins, as have the malady in less attractive forms. His own heart laughed: and that was quite enough for him.

He had no further intercourse with Spirits, but lived upon the Total Abstinence Principle, ever afterwards; and it was always said of him, that he knew how to keep Christmas well, if any man alive possessed the knowledge. May that be truly said of us, and all of us! And so, as Tiny Tim observed, God bless Us, Every One!

What might Dickens' purposes be?
- To celebrate Christmas.
- To invite the reader to celebrate Christmas.
- To ask the reader to focus on what is good in their lives and their world.
- To remind readers that God is looking after them, and that the future is therefore always full of hope.
- To make money out of a gullible public, who will lap up this sentimental fairy tale because it is Christmas.
- To persuade the middle class employers amongst his readers that they should take better care of their workers.

Any and all of these, and indeed others that you have seen for yourself will be valid. It is important to relate the structure to the author's purpose, because this will be "sophisticated" in itself. It is the same skill at A level and degree. Just as importantly, it will mark you out as different from other candidates.

Here's the question:
"You now need to think about the whole of the source.
This text is from the ending of a novel.
How has the writer structured the text to interest you as a reader? You could write about:

- what the writer focuses your attention on at the beginning
- how and why the writer changes this focus as the source develops
- any other structural features that interest you." [12 marks]

New vocabulary you will need to write about the ending of a text is "climax" and "denouement". You use "climax" to write about a peak of tension, or more typically with an ending, the last part of the crisis, which will often be a release of tension. This is also linked to the word we used when writing about conflict when looking at openings – "resolution".

The "denouement" refers to the actual ending, when the writer pulls together the different elements of the story to offer a solution that matches their purposes.

Sample paragraphs using this vocabulary

The beginning is structured with a series of very short sentences to convey Scrooge's mounting excitement about the climax he has planned for his employee, Bob: a "pay rise". The intensity of excitement is also conveyed through the structural device of repeating "he did" and "No Bob", with added emphasis from interjections such as "Oh".

However, Dickens does not want to rush the resolution, so before the denouement, Scrooge disguises his good nature by imitating his earlier meanness, "growled Scrooge...as near as he could feign it." This humour will make the reader more receptive to Dicken's message, that we should seek goodness everywhere. The denouement hammers this message home repeating "good" seven times in the penultimate paragraph.

A cynical reader might suppose...

(In blue are all my words telling the examiner that I am analysiing structure).
Practice the 10 skills by writing your own version, or try to finish this exam answer using my opening. Post it on my YouTube channel if you would like a response.

What do I have to do to get 100%?

The extract from *Brighton Rock* in the specimen paper is 621 words long. It is worth practising reading this length extract at speed. The good news for a question on structure is that it is written in 8 paragraphs. There is always a change of focus in each paragraph – that's what paragraphs denote – "dear reader," they say, "pay attention, this new paragraph means there is a slight change of Topic, Talk or Time (the 3Ts)."

So, it will be very easy to write about the changes of focus. What is more difficult is working out *why* the focus changes.

Let's look at a Damon Runyon story opening. You will notice that all the extracts I give you in this book contain difficult language. This is because you want 100%, and Paper 2 will throw some difficult 19th century texts at you. Because I want to give you an interesting shift of ending, it is slightly longer than the exemplar, at 731 words.

Please read it and work out what it is about. There will be questions at the end! These will force you to read closely. Although the exam won't do this (you will be given little footnotes to help you), such as this: 1. Rod – slang word for a gun).

These questions aren't just to test you; they are also to teach you what good readers do. Good readers find something that doesn't make sense, read the sentence before and after to get some clues about context. They then compare it to language they have met in other books, even to films about the same era, or place.

Chapter 8: Understanding the Context of Difficult Texts

The problem most students have with this is that they don't try to put their knowledge into a historical context. For example, when you read this phrase: "because he has a piece of the joint" in the text below, you will go very wrong if you think first of modern meanings of "joint". This kind of misunderstanding is natural, but if you don't read any texts that are older than 50 years, you can't get 100%. Always think about the historical context. (And of course this is also excellent practice for question 1).

"Who remembers when X Factor was just Roman sun cream?"

- Chris Turner

The Old Doll's House, by Damon Runyon

Now it seems that one cold winter night, a party of residents of Brooklyn comes across the Manhattan Bridge in an automobile wishing to pay a call on a guy by the name of Lance McGowan, who is well known to one and all along Broadway as a coming guy in the business world.

In fact, it is generally conceded that, barring accident, Lance will someday be one of the biggest guys in this country as an importer, and especially as an importer of such merchandise as fine liquors, because he is very bright, and has many good connections throughout the United States and Canada. Furthermore, Lance McGowan is a nice-looking young guy and he has plenty of ticker, although some citizens say he does not show very sound business judgment in trying to move in on Angie the Ox over in Brooklyn, as Angie the Ox is an importer himself, besides enjoying a splendid trade in other lines, including artichokes and extortion.

Of course Lance McGowan is not interested in artichokes at all, and very little in extortion, but he does not see any reason why he shall not place his imports in a thriving territory such as Brooklyn, especially as his line of merchandise is much superior to anything handled by Angie the Ox. Anyway, Angie is one of the residents of Brooklyn in the party that wishes to call on Lance McGowan, and besides Angie the party includes a guy by the name of Mockie Max, who is a very prominent character in Brooklyn, and another guy by the name of The Louse Kid, who is not so prominent, but who is considered a very promising young guy in many respects, although personally I think The Louse Kid has a very weak face.

He is supposed to be a wonderful hand with a burlap bag when anybody wishes to put somebody in such a bag, which is considered a great practical joke in Brooklyn, and in fact The Louse Kid has a burlap bag with him on the night in question, and they are figuring on putting Lance McGowan in the bag when they call on him, just for the laugh. Personally, I consider this a very crude form of humour, but then Angie the Ox and the other members of his party are very crude characters, anyway.

Well, it seems they have Lance McGowan pretty well cased, and they know that of an evening along toward ten o'clock he nearly always strolls through West Fifty-fourth street on his way to a certain spot on Park Avenue that is called the Humming Bird Club, which has a very high-toned clientele, and the reason Lance goes there is because he has a piece of the joint, and furthermore he loves to show off his shape in a tuxedo to the swell dolls.

So these residents of Brooklyn drive in their automobile along this route, and as they roll past Lance McGowan, Angie the Ox and Mockie Max let fly at Lance with a couple of sawed-offs, while The Louse Kid holds the burlap bag, figuring for all I know that Lance will be startled by the sawed-offs and will hop into the bag like a rabbit.

But Lance is by no means a sucker, and when the first blast of slugs from the sawed-offs breezes past him without hitting him, what does he do but hop over a brick wall alongside him and drop into a yard on the other side. So Angie the Ox, and Mockie Max and The Louse Kid get out of their automobile and run up close to the wall themselves because they commence figuring that if Lance McGowan starts popping at them from behind this wall, they will be taking plenty the worst of it, for of course they cannot figure Lance to be strolling about without being rodded up somewhat.

But Lance is by no means rodded up, because a rod is apt to create a bump in his shape when he has his tuxedo on, so the story really begins with Lance McGowan behind the brick wall, practically defenceless, and the reason I know this story is because Lance McGowan tells most of it to me, as Lance knows that I know his real name is Lancelot, and he feels under great obligation to me because I never mention the matter publicly.

Test your understanding and reading skills

The questions are in order of the text:

- Which city and country does this take place in?
- What is a "coming guy"?
- What is "an importer of such merchandise as fine liquors"?
- What does "plenty of ticker" mean?
- What are "artichokes"?
- What is "extortion"?
- What is a "burlap bag" for?
- What does "pretty well cased" mean?
- What is "a piece of the joint"?
- What is a "swell doll"?
- What are they doing when they "let fly at Lance with a couple of sawed-offs"?
- What are "popping" and "rodded up somewhat"?

The answers

You will get much more out of this if you try to answer by going back to the extract, because then you will see how reading what went before and what comes afterwards really helps with your guess work – this is what good readers do.

- Brooklyn and Manhattan are in New York.
- A bootlegger or gangster who is becoming more powerful.
- A bootlegger, breaking the law of the Prohibition, which made the sale of alcohol illegal in America, 1920 – 1933.
- Lots of courage.
- Vegetables probably used because it contains the word "chokes" which alludes to the violent setting implied by "extortion".
- Using threats of violence to get what you want from someone.
- To put men in, either once they are dead, or to kill them once in it. The references to humour suggest that it will be the latter.
- They have been following Lance and know his routine.
- He owns part of the business.
- A highly attractive woman.
- They shot at him with shotguns.
- Shooting and carrying a gun or guns.

Shotgun wedding:
A case of wife or death.

The structure of each paragraph of *The Old Doll's House*:

Paragraph 1
- Economical introduction of setting and main character.
- Also the use of present tense to describe the past.
- Dialect (of gangster world?)
- Authorial distance, detached from the morals of the world he describes.

Paragraph 2
- The role of the main character
- Author as witness to real events

Paragraph 3
- Introduction of other characters
- Context (of violence and corruption)
- Other perspective, showing the objectivity of the narrator

Paragraph 4
- Crisis
- Context
- Exposition (which means the back story). You will always find this relevant to the question if the source is the beginning of a book

Paragraph 5
- Introduction to the villains.
- A quick character portrait
- A sense of the setting and context (as violent)

Paragraph 6
- Establishes author's distance and disapproval
- Prediction invited with the crisis
- More in depth portrait of the villains

Paragraph 7
- Description of main character
- Description of setting which will enable the crisis to unfold

Paragraph 8
- Description of the beginning of the crisis
- Objective viewpoint of the narrator, sticking to the facts
- Ironic detachment from the events described, not becoming emotionally involved in the violence

Paragraph 9
- Description of the crisis unfolding
- Increasing the danger to the main character
- Praise of main character to invite predictions of his escape from crisis

Paragraph 10
- Detail of main character that makes escape seem impossible
- Confounding expectations, revealing that the main character survives
- With-holding how he escapes to build suspense
- Establish the narrator as an influential member of this gangster society
- Ironic, moral stance of the narrator as similar to the criminals

When you look at the list, which points will be relevant, no matter what the text?
There will always be:

- An introduction of the context
- The beginning of a novel is likely to have an exposition
- An introduction to the main character
- A presentation of a crisis
- The author's tone, or point of view

Model Answer

Ok, let's look in detail at a question on this text:

Question 3

As usual, you must highlight the key words that tell you what to write about. Because this is a new exam, it is very likely that exactly the same words will appear in the actual exam.

"You now need to think about the whole of the source.
This text is from the opening of a short story.
How has the writer structured the text to interest you as a reader? You could write about:

* what the writer focuses your attention on at the beginning
* how and why the writer changes this focus as the source develops
* any other structural features that interest you." [12 marks]

My answer

Runyon deliberately begins with an objective tone, with "Now it seems that", so that we will trust the narrator. Similarly, the second paragraph begins with "in fact" to emphasise how reliable he is – what he will tell us when he has heard things second hand.

He also structures the beginning with a specific register, a blend of slang and very formal language, almost legal in tone. So the "coming guy" and "to one and all" is immediately contrasted with "a party of residents" and "it is generally conceded that". The impression he wants us to have is of a highly educated narrator who is nevertheless completely at home in the context of "Brooklyn" and the gangster culture that sees men carrying "sawed offs".

The first four paragraphs also work as exposition, explaining this foreign culture to us, and introducing us to the main character. We infer that we are dealing with gangsters from the names of the main character's antagonist, "Angie the Ox" and this is reinforced by his link to "extortion".

The text practices delay here, as it is only at the end of the third paragraph which we discover this. This forces the reader to re-evaluate what "an importer of such merchandise as fine liquor" involves. We suspect this is criminal, however no such delay would occur to a contemporary reader, who would know that this is set in the Prohibition period.

Runyon structures the whole of the text through a contrast between the protagonist, "Lance McGowan" and his antagonists "Angie the Ox", "Mockie Max" and "The Louse Kid", who all have nicknames suggestive of mafia or gangster connections. Lance, in contrast, seems more law abiding, even though a criminal "importer".

This contrast is continued with the fact that he is not armed, while his antagonists are "rodded up somewhat". This structure develops the crisis, but the choice of casual language here helps us suppose that the protagonist will survive the attempted assassination. The threat is also deliberately minimized by introducing humour at this point, in the description of the antagonists' belief that "Lance will be startled by the sawed-offs and will hop into the bag like a rabbit".

This also serves another structural purpose. We have been introduced to the bag earlier, with The Louse Kid, who "is supposed to be a wonderful hand with a burlap bag...which is considered a great practical joke in Brooklyn". These references but only partial explanations make us keen to discover how the bag will be used, and what the "joke" is. Runyon is also preparing us for an ending where the joke will fail, through the narrator's objectivity again, where the "Kid" is "supposed" to be skilled, but may prove not to be.

The ending of the passage deliberately defuses the crisis. The narrator now tells us that Lance clearly survives because Lance "tells most of" the story "to me". Our focus therefore moves from wanting to know what happens next, to how and why the crisis is resolved. A final reason for this change of focus is also to flesh out the other main character, our narrator, who has made Lance feel "under great obligation" because he does not want the narrator to reveal his real name as "Lancelot". This achieves two purposes: letting us know that the narrator is happy to blackmail, like the criminals he writes about, and suggesting to us that we should sympathise with Lance as a morally good character, the original Lancelot being one of King Arthur's knights. [585 words]

I've included more than you could write here, because I want to teach you how to write about structure to get 100%. In 18 minutes you should be able to write a side of A4, which will be about 300 words, and I will show you how we can adapt the model to fit that.

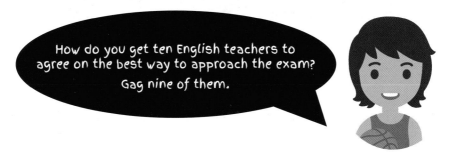

How do you get ten English teachers to agree on the best way to approach the exam? Gag nine of them.

What you should learn from this model answer

- Always begin by writing about the **beginning** – saying why the story or novel starts that way.
- Always refer to the **context** and, if possible, the **exposition**.
- Make a point about the **narrator's or the author's tone** as early as you can. This will always feel "sophisticated" to the examiner.
- Use the language of an expert throughout.
  - The choice of words of a character or of the author is always their "**register**".
  - The main character is the "**protagonist**".
  - His or her enemies are always "**antagonists**".
  - The reader always has to work things out, to "**infer**", which you must always use to discuss the effect on the reader.
  - Every story has some **conflict** in it, so we refer to it as the "**crisis**".
  - The solution to a crisis is always called a "**resolution**" – as a verb it is "**resolved**".
  - Refer to the narrator, and make sure you **distinguish between the narrator and the author**.
  - Use the **author's surname**.
- Keep referring to the word **structure**, to persuade the examiner that you are answering the question, and also to remind you not to get carried away with writing about language.
- There is very likely to be **contrast** in any text, so look for it. It is also likely that this will influence the whole of the text – make this point. Examiners will be persuaded that you have been able to have a sophisticated overview of the whole text if you **find a technique that is used throughout**. It may not have occurred to them that **most fiction texts are structured around contrast**, so you will appear much more sophisticated than you are!
- Write about the **ending** of the extract.

- If you can see clues to it, write about the ending of the chapter or the story, or to a crisis that hasn't yet been resolved in the extract.

- Use the word **"focus" sparingly** – the other candidates will be using it for each paragraph, and so it is simply a trick for you to seem more sophisticated than other candidates.

- You can **shorten quotations** by using an ellipsis to get rid of the words you don't need.

- There is **no introduction** – simply write about the purpose of the first paragraph. Even better if you spot **more than one purpose**.

- There is **no conclusion – simply write about the ending**, and if you can, the implied ending to the crisis, chapter, **story beyond the extract**.

- Ok, now comes the tricky part. Can I reduce my answer to 300 words, but still keep all of the 12 skills above?

The thief who stole a calendar? She got twelve months.

100% answer

The narrator's tone begins objectively, with "now it seems that", and "in fact" so he appears reliable: we will trust him.

He deliberately starts with a specific register, blending slang and a formal, legal-like tone. So "coming guy" and "to one and all" contrasts with "a party of residents" and "generally conceded that", portraying the narrator's comfort in the gangster context of "Brooklyn".

The first half is exposition, introducing the protagonist, and the gangster context through their names: one antagonist is "Angie the Ox" which is reinforced by "extortion". The whole text is a contrast between the protagonist, "Lance McGowan" and his antagonists, including "Mockie Max" and "The Louse Kid", who all have nicknames suggestive of gangsters, while conversely, Lance seems more law abiding, though a criminal "importer".

Consequently, he is unarmed, while his antagonists are "rodded up somewhat", developing the crisis. The casual "somewhat" implies the protagonist will survive the attempted assassination. Similarly, the narrator's joke that "Lance will be startled by the sawed-offs and will hop into the bag like a rabbit" implies this.

The repeated, partial explanations of the "bag" and the "Kid", who "is supposed to be a wonderful hand with a burlap bag... considered a great practical joke in Brooklyn" make us keen to understand the "joke", foreshadowing an ending where the joke will fail, as the "Kid" is "supposed" to be skilled, but may prove not to be.

The ending defuses the crisis. Lance survives because Lance "tells most of" the story "to me", so we focus on how the crisis is resolved, thereby portraying our narrator as a blackmailer, threatening to reveal Lance's real name as "Lancelot" unless he reveals what happened. We therefore sympathise with Lance as a moral character, like the original knight, Lancelot.

(In blue are all the words that refer specifically to structure. Other students will keep writing about the change in focus, which is going to be boring for the examiner and the student. If you use the vocabulary above, you will always keep thinking about the writer's purpose in this structure, and you will easily attain at least a level 7) [293 words]

What this means for you

Now, it shouldn't surprise you that it took me longer to reduce this than to write it in the first place. This is a wonderful exercise if you want to get 100%, because it will train you to say more in fewer words. To explain how I did it would bore you – simply compare the two and examine the changes. Below is a checklist of skills I try to teach my students so they can do this:

- Get rid of any repetition.
- Delete any words you can, so that the writing still has the same meaning.
- Switch the word order, so that the main idea comes earlier.
- Use connectives to link ideas, and get rid of phrases that were linking them.
- Get rid of words at the beginning of a sentence, use a comma, and then a verb ending in 'ing'.
- Link more ideas together with commas (although you must be careful not to link to a whole sentence – instead delete some words from the next sentence so that it only makes sense linked to your first idea).
- Choose vocabulary that replaces more than one word.

You will learn a lot by going back over both versions of my answer and trying to identify where 1 – 7 have occurred. Then you will learn even more by trying it with your own exam practice. This means that sometimes you will take much longer than the time allowed, to try to get a 100% answer. Then chop it down so you learn to write much more informative sentences.

Because this will lead to your eventually writing longer answers that go well beyond the A* or 9. For example, I could still get full marks simply by removing a few sentences or paragraphs from my longer answer – this would still leave enough ideas to gain full marks.

Model answer

Runyon deliberately begins with an objective tone, with "Now it seems that", so that we will trust the narrator. Similarly, the second paragraph begins with "in fact" to emphasise how reliable he is – what he will tell us when he has heard things second hand.

He also structures the beginning with a specific register, a blend of slang and very formal language, almost legal in tone. So the "coming guy" and "to one and all" is immediately contrasted with "a party of residents" and "it is generally conceded that". The impression he wants us to have is of a highly educated narrator who is never the less completely at home in the context of "Brooklyn" and the gangster culture that sees men carrying "sawed offs".

The first four paragraphs also work as exposition, introducing us to the main character. We infer that we are dealing with gangsters from the names of the main character's antagonist, "Angie the Ox" and this is reinforced by his link to "extortion".

Runyon structures the whole of the text through a contrast between the protagonist, "Lance McGowan" and his antagonists "Angie the Ox", "Mockie Max" and "The Louse Kid", who all have nicknames suggestive of mafia or gangster connections.

This contrast is continued with the fact that he is not armed, while his antagonists are "rodded up somewhat". This structure develops the crisis, but the choice of casual language here helps us suppose that the protagonist will survive the attempted assassination. The threat is also deliberately minimized by introducing humour at this point, in the description of the antagonists' belief that "Lance will be startled by the sawed-offs and will hop into the bag like a rabbit".

The ending deliberately defuses the crisis. Lance clearly survives because Lance "tells most of" the story "to me". Our focus therefore moves from wanting to know what happens next, to how and why the crisis is resolved.

This is 320 words, simply by chopping words out of my model answer, and changing nothing else. Although it is a weaker answer than the two models above, it does have some sophisticated ideas relating to structure. The italicized paragraphs probably contain points that other candidates will not write about, and therefore this response is still likely to be graded at 8 or 9. If you don't have time to work through all the techniques I have taught you in this section, it will be worth imitating my paragraphs. Go to project Gutenberg (at www.gutenberg.org) and look at another Damon Runyon short story, and try to write similar paragraphs about it. Post them on my YouTube channel if you would like some feedback.

Chapter 9: Paper 1, Question 4

Just tell me what to do

- Highlight the key words in the question which tell you what to look for
- Highlight in the margin of the part of the text you are told to look at
- Agree or disagree with the statement straight away, in one sentence. It is usually easiest to agree
- Find quotations relevant to the first bullet point
- Write about these and relate them to the key word in the opinion of the question
- Embed these in your sentences
- Identify what technique is being used and name it
- Develop an argument by moving chronologically through the test, explaining how each new quotation adds to the impression you are discussing
- If you can see moments where the stated opinion is wrong, explain these. They will show you are being evaluative.
- Use tentative language, like 'perhaps', 'it appears,' 'might' etc

What does the question look like?

Focus this part of your answer on the second part of the source from line 16 to the end.

A student, having read this section of the text, said: "This part of the text, explaining what Draco is doing, shows how happy and free he feels. It's as if we feel his excitement." To what extent do you agree?

In your response, you could:
- consider your own impressions of how Draco feels
- evaluate how the writer creates a happy atmosphere
- support your opinions with references to the text. [20 marks]

Some problems with the question

Problem 1: Deciding whether you should agree or disagree with the opinion

In this question you will always be given an opinion which the examiner has invented. Like this one, they will probably pretend it comes from a student. In the examiner's mind, they are doing you a favour. By giving you a point of view, they hope you won't sit there staring at the page, but will have something to write about – it is simply designed to help you start writing.

There are two problems with this though. There are no marks for agreeing or disagreeing with the opinion the examiners give you. The examiner does not care what you think! So just start writing. On balance, it is usually easier to say that you partly agree straight away.

Problem 2: Deciding whether to quote

The question will be worded like this:

"In your response, you could:
• support your opinions with references to the text."

This is simply wrong. You **MUST** support your ideas with reference to the text in all of question 1 – 4 on this paper.

Problem 3: Disagreeing with the statement

Now, there is a third problem with the opinion the examiner will give you.

Here is the relevant part of the question:
"This part of the text, explaining what Draco is doing, shows how happy and free he feels. It's as if we feel his excitement."

You might answer the question by writing about how happy and free Draco is, or not happy, or not free. It is this second part of your response that is the problem. The marks are available for your evaluation **of the effect on the reader**. This means you must write about what the writer is doing, rather than what the writer is not doing. You could waste a lot of time writing about how you think Draco feels, arguing he does not feel "free" but not write about any of the other things Draco is feeling.

Problem 4: The question does not ask you to write about the writer's methods but the mark scheme does!

Now, worst of all, even if you did write about what Draco is feeling, you might still not get the marks. This is because this question will never ask you to write about your "**perceptive understanding of writer's methods**". These are the words of the mark scheme – you MUST write about the writer's methods.

You need to infer the need to write about methods from:
"Evaluate how the writer creates a happy atmosphere".

"I'm learning the hokey cokey. Not all of it. But I've got the ins and outs."
- Iain Stirling

What does the mark scheme say?

You will:
- Evaluate (e.g. say why you only partly agree with the statement)
- Write in detail
- Be perceptive
- Write about the effect on the reader
- Have a range of quotations
- Be convincing
- Be critical of the statement (e.g. say why you only partly agree with it)

Exam Tactics

You must learn the subject terminology in this section. No shortcuts – this is not a hairdressers. No excuses – the dog didn't eat your revision

There are obvious features which you will always look for:

- **Simile, metaphor, personification, alliteration, sibilance, onomatopoeia**; these are the main forms of **imagery** or **symbolism**.
- Then we have structural features, that also count as language features: **contrast, juxtaposition, repetition**.
- Next we have features that reveal the author's, or narrator's, or main character's tone: **register, allusion, reference.**

Chapter 10: Glossary of Terms

Simile is where you use the word "like" or "as" to make a comparison, describing why one thing is like another.

- His smile was like honey, sweet, alluring, promising a lifetime of plenty.
- The moment passed, like a rescue ship, and she was left alone, all alone, the sole survivor of the wreck of her marriage.
- The snake was as beautiful as a well told lie. It waited for the gullible dog.

Metaphor is where you make a comparison, by saying one thing is, or was something else.

- The moment passed, like a rescue ship, and she was left alone, all alone, the sole survivor of the wreck of her marriage.
- The music played silver notes, and the singers voice was a diamond, a gift of love.
- Summer blazed in the wood, colour exploding up the tree trunks, **licking the branches with warmth**.

I went out on a date with a simile. I don't know what I metaphor.

Personification is where you use a simile or, more often, a metaphor to describe something that is not human, with characteristics, which are human – like a person.

- The inscrutable police car sat motionless as a judge weighing up a death sentence.
- The sword quivered with joy, ready to punch, slash and stab.
- The TV winked open its giant eye, inviting me to get lost within.

Alliteration is where the sounds of consonants are the same in words that are close together. Usually, but not exclusively, the sounds will be at the beginning of words.

- Creeping carefully, the dog tracked the scent of my cooking, and pounced as I poured the gravy.
- "Forget the phone, you fool, it's bugged, and we're so busted."
- "It's not a party, it's a get together," complained Candace, while Phineas and Ferb laughed loud and long.

Sibilance is alliteration of the 'S' sound.

- The moment passed, like a rescue ship, and she was left alone, all alone, the sole survivor of the wreck of her marriage.
- Soft waves swept the shore, and the sand whispered like a waking lover.
- The pen scratched and scribbled, never stopping to make sense.

Onomatopoeia is when words recreate sounds. Usually they are spelt in such a way that they sound like the sounds they are describing. Note that alliteration can have an onomatopoeic effect.

- Soft waves swept the shore, and the sand whispered like a waking lover.
- The pen scratched and scribbled, never stopping to make sense.
- The sword quivered with joy, ready to punch, slash and stab.

Imagery uses descriptive features like those listed above to recreate one or more of the senses. Don't just think of it as visual, but also sound, smell, taste, texture.

- The blue sky was bright with hope.
- The bed fought back, each lump in the mattress was a fist, both pillows slick with sweat like a boxer's chest.
- I stepped off the plane, tasted the heat of the sun, an exotic spice to the main course of my holiday to come.

Symbolism is when something that stands for or represents something else, often an idea.
In *Little Red Riding Hood*, her name is symbolic of sexual experience, the Wolf is symbolic of male sexual desire which is portrayed as destructive. The mother's instruction to stay on the path is symbolic of following society's rules, and in particular preserving Little Red Riding Hood's virginity. The woodcutter who kills the wolf is symbolic of either the father's protection, or the finding of a true partner, depending on how you want to read the story. Now, you might not read the story this way at all, which is fine. However, you will need to provide your own symbolic interpretation – deal with the symbolism and you will ace level 7 and beyond.

Contrast is where two things are put close together in order to emphasise the difference between them.

- The parental expectation that Jack is a useless son who has reduced them to poverty when selling their cow for beans, is contrasted with the resolution where the courageous, resourceful and lucky Jack raises the family to riches.
- The fate of the first two pigs, who built their houses quickly, is contrasted with the fate of the younger but wiser pig who builds his house of bricks.
- The warmth and promise of spring is contrasted with the melancholy and cold of winter.

Juxtaposition is when two things are put close together in order to emphasise the difference between them.

- "Give us a pound, mister," said the beggar, scrolling through the internet on his phone.
- The mother, tortured with pain, now smiled beatifically, while the baby, newly released, screamed incessantly.
- While the battle raged, the generals sat behind the front lines, drinking beers and stuffing three course meals.

Repetition is the repeating of a word, phrase, or idea. This can be done to emphasise, to create a rhythm or tone, or to reveal a contrast or comparison.

Register in linguistics, a **register** is a variety of a language used for a particular purpose or in a particular setting.

What words give this the register of colloquial, American teenage language?
"(Candace runs out to the backyard, she stares in shock upon seeing the rollercoaster, along with horror music)

Candace: Phineas, what is this?!

Phineas: Do you like it?

Candace: Ooh, I'm gonna tell Mom, and when she sees what you're doing, you are going down. (runs off) Down! Down! Down! D-O-W-N, down!"

Which words deal with the idea of writing a novel?

"In my mind, I continually entertain myself with fragments of narrative, dialogue and plot twists but as soon as I'm in front of a blank page, they evaporate. I feel stuck. Sometimes I think I should give up, but I have convinced myself that if I can find a way to write more freely and suppress my inner critic, I could finally finish that first draft."

It was my first day at a new school. I walked in.
The teacher said, "sit there for the present."
So I sat there all day, getting more and more disappointed.
After sitting there all day, I still hadn't had my present.
On the plus side, sitting in the staff room all day was nice.

Allusion is a brief and indirect reference to a person, place, thing or idea of historical, cultural, literary or political significance. It therefore depends on the reader being well-read.

- Jose Mourihno attacks the game like a man who has been told that no man born of woman can ever defeat him. Unfortunately, it may be that Pep Guardiola was born by caesarean section. (Check out *Macbeth* for the allusion).

- Donald Trump loves ice cream. Forget Ben and Jerry's, he only likes Walls. (Ask a Mexican for the allusion)

- 2B or not 2B? Picasso picked up his pencil and wondered whether to paint or write a play. (You need to know something about Hamlet and the names of pencils for the allusions)

Reference is to mention or allude to something.

Synesthesia is a figurative use of words that intends to draw out a response from readers stimulating more than one of the senses.

From *The Great Gatsby* by F. Scott Fitzgerald: "The lights grow brighter as the earth lurches away from the sun, and now the orchestra is playing yellow cocktail music, and the opera of voices pitches a higher key." Here the colour yellow invites us to imagine a happy sound to the music.

From Oscar Wilde's *An Ideal Husband*: "I believe they have got a mauve Hungarian band that plays mauve Hungarian music." The music sounds dull and tuneless, as mauve is a dull and muted form of purple.

In the song Red, by Taylor Swift, "Losing him was blue like I'd never known/Missing him was dark grey all alone." The colours reflect the singer's emotions. "Loving him was red." See – Little Red Riding Hood lives on!

You need to practise using all these words accurately. Then you need to practise memorizing them, so that you don't have to think about them – they need to be on the tip of your tongue, and on the tip of your pen in the exam.

What do I have to do to get 100%?

Since AQA's sample papers use 20th century texts, where the author did not die at least 70 years ago, they are copyrighted. Consequently, I have adapted a question and mark scheme in the next chapter

"My brother and friends spend all of their time floating out at sea. Well, boys will be buoys."

- Bec Hill

Chapter 11: Sample Texts for Paper 1

You can find both of these novels, their full texts, on Project Gutenberg. You should visit it to read all kinds of texts that are more than 70 years old – this will make you an expert in English.

The 39 Steps, by John Buchan

Chapter one: The Man Who Died

Here was I, thirty-seven years old, sound in wind and limb, with enough money to have a good time, yawning my head off all day. I had just about settled to clear out and get back to the veld, for I was the best bored man in the United Kingdom.

That afternoon I had been worrying my brokers about investments to give my mind something to work on, and on my way home I turned into my club—rather a pot-house, which took in Colonial members. I had a long drink, and read the evening papers. They were full of the row in the Near East, and there was an article about Karolides, the Greek Premier. I rather fancied the chap. From all accounts he seemed the one big man in the show; and he played a straight game too, which was more than could be said for most of them. I gathered that they hated him pretty blackly in Berlin and Vienna, but that we were going to stick by him, and one paper said that he was the only barrier between Europe and Armageddon. I remember wondering if I could get a job in those parts. It struck me that Albania was the sort of place that might keep a man from yawning.

About six o'clock I went home, dressed, dined at the Cafe Royal, and turned into a music hall. It was a silly show, all capering women and monkey-faced men, and I did not stay long. The night was fine and clear as I walked back to the flat I had hired near Portland Place. The crowd surged past me on the pavements, busy and chattering, and I envied the people for having something to do. These shop-girls and clerks and dandies and policemen had some interest in life that kept them going. I gave half-a-crown to a beggar because I saw him yawn; he was a fellow-sufferer. At Oxford Circus I looked up into the spring sky and I made a vow. I would give the Old Country another day to fit me into something; if nothing happened, I would take the next boat for the Cape.

My flat was the first floor in a new block behind Langham Place. There was a common staircase, with a porter and a liftman at the entrance, but there was no restaurant or anything of that sort, and each flat was quite shut off from the others. I hate servants on the premises, so I had a fellow to look after me who came in by the day. He arrived before eight o'clock every morning and used to depart at seven, for I never dined at home.

I was just fitting my key into the door when I noticed a man at my elbow. I had not seen him approach, and the sudden appearance made me start. He was a slim man, with a short brown beard and small, gimlety blue eyes. I recognized him as the occupant of a flat on the top floor, with whom I had passed the time of day on the stairs.

'Can I speak to you?' he said. 'May I come in for a minute?' He was steadying his voice with an effort, and his hand was pawing my arm.

I got my door open and motioned him in. No sooner was he over the threshold than he made a dash for my back room, where I used to smoke and write my letters. Then he bolted back.

'Is the door locked?' he asked feverishly, and he fastened the chain with his own hand.

'I'm very sorry,' he said humbly. 'It's a mighty liberty, but you looked the kind of man who would understand. I've had you in my mind all this week when things got troublesome. Say, will you do me a good turn?'

'I'll listen to you,' I said. 'That's all I'll promise.' I was getting worried by the antics of this nervous little chap.

There was a tray of drinks on a table beside him, from which he filled himself a stiff whisky-and-soda. He drank it off in three gulps, and cracked the glass as he set it down.

'Pardon,' he said, 'I'm a bit rattled tonight. You see, I happen at this moment to be dead.'
[717 words]

Before you study this question, use the checklist we met on page 4, and see if you can use it to write about this passage.

Call of the Wild, by Jack London

Chapter one: Into the Primitive

Buck did not read the newspapers, or he would have known that trouble was brewing, not alone for himself, but for every tidewater dog, strong of muscle and with warm, long hair, from Puget Sound to San Diego. Because men, groping in the Arctic darkness, had found a yellow metal, and because steamship and transportation companies were booming the find, thousands of men were rushing into the Northland. These men wanted dogs, and the dogs they wanted were heavy dogs, with strong muscles by which to toil, and furry coats to protect them from the frost.

Buck lived at a big house in the sun-kissed Santa Clara Valley. Judge Miller's place, it was called. It stood back from the road, half hidden among the trees, through which glimpses could be caught of the wide cool veranda that ran around its four sides. The house was approached by gravelled driveways which wound about through wide-spreading lawns and under the interlacing boughs of tall poplars. At the rear things were on even a more spacious scale than at the front. There were great stables, where a dozen grooms and boys held forth, rows of vine-clad servants' cottages, an endless and orderly array of outhouses, long grape arbors, green pastures, orchards, and berry patches. Then there was the pumping plant for the artesian well, and the big cement tank where Judge Miller's boys took their morning plunge and kept cool in the hot afternoon.

And over this great demesne Buck ruled. Here he was born, and here he had lived the four years of his life. It was true, there were other dogs, there could not but be other dogs on so vast a place, but they did not count. They came and went, resided in the populous kennels, or lived obscurely in the recesses of the house after the fashion of Toots, the Japanese pug, or Ysabel, the Mexican hairless, —strange creatures that rarely put nose out of doors or set foot to ground. On the other hand, there were the fox terriers, a score of them at least, who yelped fearful promises at Toots and Ysabel looking out of the windows at them and protected by a legion of housemaids armed with brooms and mops.

But Buck was neither house-dog nor kennel-dog. The whole realm was his. He plunged into the swimming tank or went hunting with the Judge's sons; he escorted Mollie and Alice, the Judge's daughters, on long twilight or early morning rambles; on wintry nights he lay at the Judge's feet before the roaring library fire; he carried the Judge's grandsons on his back, or rolled them in the grass, and guarded their footsteps through wild adventures down to the fountain in the stable yard, and even beyond, where the paddocks were, and the berry patches. Among the terriers he stalked imperiously, and Toots and Ysabel he utterly ignored, for he was king, —king over all creeping, crawling, flying things of Judge Miller's place, humans included.

His father, Elmo, a huge St. Bernard, had been the Judge's inseparable companion, and Buck bid fair to follow in the way of his father. He was not so large, —he weighed only one hundred and forty pounds, —for his mother, Shep, had been a Scotch shepherd dog. Nevertheless, one hundred and forty pounds, to which was added the dignity that comes of good living and universal respect, enabled him to carry himself in right royal fashion. During the four years since his puppyhood he had lived the life of a sated aristocrat; he had a fine pride in himself, was even a trifle egotistical, as country gentlemen sometimes become because of their insular situation. But he had saved himself by not becoming a mere pampered house-dog. Hunting and kindred outdoor delights had kept down the fat and hardened his muscles; and to him, as to the cold-tubbing races, the love of water had been a tonic and a health preserver.

And this was the manner of dog Buck was in in the fall of 1897, when the Klondike strike dragged men from all the world into the frozen North. But Buck did not read the newspapers, and he did not know that Manuel, one of the gardener's helpers, was an undesirable acquaintance. Manuel had one besetting sin. He loved to play Chinese lottery. Also, in his gambling, he had one besetting weakness— faith in a system; and this made his damnation certain. For to play a system requires money, while the wages of a gardener's helper do not lap over the needs of a wife and numerous progeny. [766 words]

I've deliberately chosen texts that are a bit unusual, as I am trying to lure you into reading early 20th century texts. You will get to grips with much more complex sentences and vocabulary than modern novels, and you will be fully prepared for the exam.

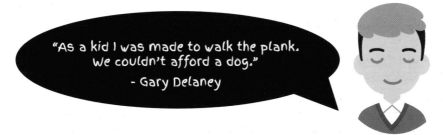

"As a kid I was made to walk the plank. We couldn't afford a dog."
- Gary Delaney

Find the techniques in these quotations I've taken from the passage
Among the terriers he stalked imperiously, and Toots and Ysabel he utterly ignored, for he was king, — king over all creeping, crawling, flying things of Judge Miller's place, humans included.

Hunting and kindred outdoor delights had kept down the fat and hardened his muscles; and to him, as to the cold-tubbing races, the love of water had been a tonic and a health preserver.
And this was the manner dog Buck was in in the fall of 1897, when the Klondike strike dragged men

from all the world into the frozen North. But Buck did not read the newspapers, and he did not know that Manuel, one of the gardener's helpers, was an undesirable acquaintance.

Did you spot:
- The metaphor, that he "was king"?
- The repetition of "king".
- The allusion to Genesis in the Bible, where like Adam and Eve, he ruled over every "creeping" "thing".
- The alliteration of "creeping, crawling".
- The anthropomorphism of the second paragraph, describing Buck as a man.
- The allusion to falling, reminiscent of failure, or of The Fall of Adam and Eve, in "fall of 1897".
- The personification of Klondike strike which "dragged men from all over".
- The alliteration and internal rhyme of "Klondike strike".
- The use of contrast of "the frozen North" compared to the land Buck has grown up on.
- The contrast of Buck's sense of certainty with the warning, "But Buck did not read".
- The allusion to Buck's intelligence – London did not write "could not read", as though to suggests that he simply chose not to learn to read.
- The contrast of Buck's intelligence to his ignorance, "and he did not know that".

Don't worry if you didn't find many of these. You don't need a dozen quotations, as you only have 30 minutes in which to write. My point, instead, is that once you get used to finding these features in texts, you will find the exam easy. It is unlikely that you will need to write about more than 10 quotations for 100%. In the AQA exemplar on Hale, which indicates the quality, not length of writing, the examiner uses 6 quotations in 238 words. This is about one every 40 words. However, several of these are simply one word quotations. You can beat this just using the small parts of the passage I have forced you to look at.

Look at the rest of the passage and test yourself – how many more can you find?

You will quickly get to the stage where you can find 15 - 20 quotations in the whole passage, and in the exam, you will only need 10.

What you should do to revise this:
- Look at the 12 points that I have found. For each one, try to write about why Jack London has portrayed Buck this way. Link your answer to the question.
- Post your answers on my YouTube channel if you would like me to comment on it.
- Practise the skills of cutting down the words, as I showed you earlier.

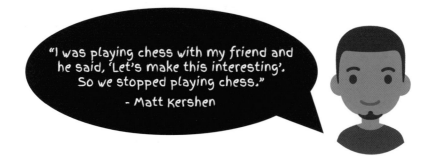

What does the examiner really want?

Often students worry that they don't know how to start. This is death in the exam. One minute spent wondering how to start is one minute not getting marks. That's probably one mark gone – my maximum mark is now only 99%. Most students wait more than a minute, and lose even more marks. Instead, my advice is just to start. Start with the first thing written about your character (it is highly likely that question 4 will always be about a character). You simply ask yourself:

How is the writer trying to influence how I think or feel about this character?

This is a 20-mark question which you know means you have 30 minutes. You need to keep practising writing under exam conditions. My rough guide would be that you ought to be able to write 450 words in that time, or a side and a half of A4. My sample beginning is 301 words, so 20 minutes' worth of writing.

You would never write this much on one paragraph in the exam. But I would encourage you to write like this in your revision. That's why it is here. It will develop your confidence that ideas can be found everywhere. This will liberate you during the exam, because you will then be able to choose what you consider the best points, the ones that will show you as "sophisticated".

Model answer

Here is my made up question for *Call of the Wild*, which you will see is very closely based on the specimen paper:

Focus this part of your answer on the second part of the source from line 18 (I have put these in italics for you – the exam won't) to the end.

A student, having read this section of the text, said: "This part of the text, explaining what Buck is doing, shows how safe and superior he feels. It reminds me of pride before a fall."

To what extent do you agree? In your response, you could:
- consider your own impressions of how Buck feels
- evaluate how the writer creates an unsafe atmosphere
- support your opinions with references to the text.

The **narrator** uses a **register** that suggests power, so that "Buck ruled". He is also **anthropomorphized** as a land owner, owning a "great demesne". The use of "great" **as opposed to** large reflects Buck's sense of his own worth. London contrasts this greatness with vanity, so that we might see Buck's vanity, believing other dogs "did not count".

The other dogs are far less important to him because of their address, so they "lived obscurely in the recesses of the house". This **portrays** Buck as a bit of snob. London wants us to both admire and dislike Buck, so that he is slightly **racist**, dismissing the other dogs as foreign, "Japanese" and "Mexican", and by **referring** to them as "creatures". Of course, this also **suggests** how human-like he sees himself, so he **contrasts** himself as not a "creature". **We** are encouraged to marvel at his intelligence, so that he **seems to** be having a **dialogue** with himself: "It was true, there were other dogs", **as though** he is questioning his own vanity and self-importance.

However, so grand is his vision of his own greatness, that he sees himself as superior to the servants, who are **described** in **metaphor** to show their subservience, as "a legion of housemaids armed with brooms and mops". This also hints at **sexism**, as no male servants are dismissed as faceless, part of this "legion" and the housemaids are **linked** to the female dog, "Ysabel" and the **probably** female "Toots".

This allusion to protection and being "armed" also **prepares us** for Buck's lack of safety – he will need protection, but does not realise that he is unsafe. This is even more apparent when **we consider** that his legions are made up of women and yapping terriers who can only communicate "fearful promises" and whose weapons are only made of wood. [304 words]

The words in bold indicate the writer's methods, and the kind of vocabulary that will convince the examiners that you are an expert in writing about literature. Notice too the words that suggest a tentative interpretation, "**seems, as though, probably**". This suggests to the examiner that you are considering many possibilities and interpretations, because you are a "sophisticated" reader.

The examiner's exemplar for the specimen papers is written in the first person. I have deliberately avoided this – referring to yourself as "us" and "we" presents you as the expert reader. "I" invites a reader to disagree with you. "We" invites the reader to agree with you.

Notice again that I don't write in PEE paragraphs: instead each sentence contains at least two of point, evidence, explanation. The only rule is that there must always be a linking explanation.

"I needed a password eight characters long so I picked Snow White and the Seven Dwarves."
- Nick Helm

Let's code it to see what I mean:

Model Answer:
The narrator uses a register **that suggests power, so that** "Buck ruled". He is also anthropomorphized as a land owner, owning a "great demesne". The use of "great" **as opposed to large reflects** Buck's sense of his own worth. London contrasts this greatness with vanity, **so that we might see Buck's vanity, believing other dogs** "did not count".

The other dogs are far less important to him **because of their address, so they** "lived obscurely in the recesses of the house". **This portrays Buck as a bit of snob**. London wants us to both admire and dislike Buck, **so that he is slightly racist, dismissing the other dogs as foreign,** "Japanese" and "Mexican", **and by referring to them as** "creatures". **Of course, this also suggests how human-like he sees himself, so** he contrasts himself as not a "creature". We are encouraged to marvel at his intelligence, **so that he seems to be having a dialogue with himself**: "It was true, there were other dogs", **as though he is questioning his own vanity and self-importance**.

Key:
Point
Evidence
Explanation

I hope you can see that you are still writing using PEE, but you are no longer worried about the order of point and evidence. Explanation always comes last, unless you are linking to a new explanation. Every point still has evidence to back it up, and each point is also explained. But, these ideas are linked together much more fluently, not clumsily, like a PEE paragraph.

See if you can do this one for yourself:

However, so grand is his vision of his own greatness, that he sees himself as superior to the servants, who are **described** in **metaphor** to show their subservience, "a legion of housemaids armed with brooms and mops". This also hints at **sexism**, as no male servants are dismissed as faceless, part of this "legion" and the housemaids are **linked** to the female dog, "Ysabel" and the **probably** female "Toots". This allusion to protection and being "armed" also **prepares us** for Buck's lack of safety – he will need protection, but does not realise that he is unsafe. This is even more apparent when **we consider** that his legions are made up of women, yapping terriers who can only communicate "fearful promises" and whose weapons are only made of wood.

The magic finger (or where I found my quotations)
And over this great demesne <u>Buck ruled</u>. Here he was born, and here he had lived the four years of his life. <u>It was true, there were other dogs</u>, there could not but be other dogs on so vast a place, but they did not count. They came and went, resided in the populous kennels, or <u>lived obscurely in the recesses of the house</u> after the fashion of Toots, the Japanese pug, or Ysabel, the Mexican hairless, —strange <u>creatures</u> that rarely put nose out of doors or set foot to ground. On the other hand, there were the fox terriers, a score of them at least, who yelped fearful promises at Toots and Ysabel looking out of the windows at them and <u>protected by a legion of housemaids armed with brooms and mops</u>.

This is what I mean by 'the magic finger'. If you close your eyes, and just stab the text, that sentence will magically have a method in it about which you can write. You don't have to go looking for these methods. They are everywhere!

One of the skills I want my students to learn is that they are in charge in an exam. Writers genuinely think about every sentence they write, often every word. When I wrote *The Slightly Awesome Teacher*, I redrafted it four times, and cut over 66,000 words. All writers do this. You should therefore be confident that there probably will be a quotation that you can write about in each sentence, probably, as in my example, each line.

The cross-eyed teacher lost her job.
She couldn't control her pupils.

What skills have we repeated from question 3 in question 4?
There are 8. As you work through the skills of each question, you will find that you get better and better at the exam as a whole, because these skills keep recurring.

- Make a point about the narrator's or the author's tone as early as you can. This will always feel "sophisticated" to the examiner.
- Use the language of an expert throughout.
    - The choice of words of a character or of the author is always their "register".
    - The main character is the "protagonist". His or her enemies are always "antagonists".
    - The reader always has to work things out, to "infer", which you must always use to discuss the effect on the reader.
    - Every story has some conflict in it, so we refer to it as the "crisis".
    - The solution to a crisis is always called a "resolution" – as a verb it is "resolved".
    - Refer to the narrator, and make sure you distinguish between the narrator and the author.

- Use the author's surname.

- There is very likely to be contrast in any text, so look for it. It is also likely that this will influence the whole of the text – make this point. Examiners will be persuaded that you have been able to have a sophisticated overview of the whole text if you find a technique that is used throughout. It may not have occurred to them that most fiction texts are structured around contrast, so you will appear much more sophisticated than you are!

- Write about the ending of the extract.

- If you can see clues to it, write about the ending of the chapter or the story, or to a crisis that hasn't yet been resolved in the extract.

- You can shorten quotations by using an ellipsis to get rid of the words you don't need.

- There is no introduction, simply write about the purpose of the first paragraph. Even better if you spot more than one purpose.

- There is no conclusion, simply write about the ending, and if you can, the implied ending to the crisis, chapter, story beyond the extract.

Chapter 12: Paper 1, Section B

The writing question: to describe and narrate

In question 5 you will be offered a choice of two questions. These are the three types of combination you might get:

- Write a story, OR write a description
- Write a story based on this picture, OR write a different story
- Write a description based on this photograph, OR write a different description

You will always be given a picture. This doesn't mean that you have to stick to it. You'll see what I mean later.

You must be prepared to describe, and write a story. The exam paper will tell you to "spend about 45 minutes on this section".

The question will also tell you "of the need to plan your answer".

Just tell me what to do

5 minute plan:
- Spend one minute drawing your scene really quickly and messily
- In one minute, write words that give you sounds and textures
- Label each bit with adjectives and/or adverbs: maximum of a minute
- Write what these are similar to (this will give you interesting similes, metaphors and personification): maximum of two minutes

Write:
- Start each sentence in a different way
- Show off with your vocabulary
- Show off with your control of sentences
    Really short sentences for tension
    A curtailed sentence (without a verb) for emphasis or drama
    Long, complex and convoluted sentence to layer description and information
- Show off with your control of paragraphing
    A short, one sentence paragraph
    A long one sentence paragraph
    Mirror the sentence structure of one paragraph in another
- Show off with your control of punctuation
- Commas, colons, semi-colons, dashes, brackets
- Write an ending which refers back to an earlier idea or makes the reader question what next

- Use all the techniques of SOAPAIMS (most schools use this mnemonic)

  Similes
  Onomatopoeia
  Alliteration
  Personification
  Adjectives
  Imagery
  Metaphor
  Senses

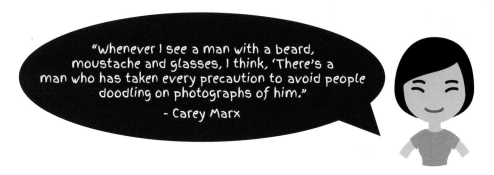

"Whenever I see a man with a beard, moustache and glasses, I think, 'There's a man who has taken every precaution to avoid people doodling on photographs of him."
- Carey Marx

What does the question look like?

Your school or college is asking students to contribute some creative writing for its Facebook page.

Either: Write a description suggested by this picture: (here you will get a picture)

Or: Describe an occasion when you felt under confident or challenged. Write about your thoughts and feelings at that time.

(24 marks for content and organization and 16 marks for technical accuracy) [40 marks]

Will it be an exciting picture? Almost, definitely not. Will it be an interesting topic to describe? No, expect boring. The examiner will think it is interesting. However, many of you will not have faced interesting challenges and so may feel stuck. Many more of you will have faced interesting challenges – dyslexia, immigration, moving schools, close friends betraying you, friends and family dying, someone special with cancer, the death of a pet, the coach doesn't believe in you, you think you are ugly and no one will find you attractive, you only feel confident when you are drunk, you are convinced your parents can't be your real parents – that you must be adopted, etc, but you don't realise these are real challenges. And just as many of you will think, "no, that's personal/embarrassing/too emotional – I won't write about that." But you really should! Even if you don't, this guide will still help you.

So, I have some solutions for you in this section of the guide.

What does the mark scheme say?

To get in the top band, your writing needs to be "compelling and convincing". This is marked in two areas:

Assessment Objective 4: Content
- Register is convincing
- Everything matches your purpose
- Ambitious vocabulary with lots of linguistic devices

Assessment Objective 5: Organisation
- Inventive structural features
- Convincing and complex ideas
- Fluently-linked paragraphs

There are 24 marks available for showing those skills.

Next you are marked for the accuracy and quality of your sentences and punctuation.
Assessment objective 6: technical accuracy
- Sentence demarcation is consistently accurate
- Wide range of punctuation used accurately
- A wide range of appropriate sentence forms
- Uses Standard English
- Control of complex grammar and complex sentences
- Accurate spelling, including ambitious vocabulary
- Extensive and ambitious vocabulary

There are 16 marks for showing these skills.

How can you make this easy to remember?
I always find it best to simplify mark schemes. What is it you have to do to meet all of these, without having to think about all of them (which would be impossible).

Your checklist
- Use an imaginative structure
- Use lots of techniques, and use them originally
- Show off with vocabulary
- Show off with different types of sentences
- Show off with a range of punctuation

You will learn several ways of doing all of these in these pages.

Model answer
Imagine the descriptive question is based on this picture:

Something wasn't right. The van didn't belong here. It stood out, orange in the sun's haze, and seemingly brand new. Although its windows were clean and unbroken, in dramatic contrast to the house, I could see no one inside. Yet the engine growled menacingly, like some hunting leopard, crouched in the scorched grass.

Standing miserably beside the VW was a dilapidated house, squashed and ripped, a toddler's discarded Christmas present chucked away as soon as opened. The windows, cracked into sharp and jagged pieces, looked out at me like a miserable face. Its brickwork appeared shoddy, built by workmen who knew they wouldn't be paid much for doing a good job. One sad door hung on its hinges, groaning like a teenager watching a black and white film. Above, the roof sagged and decayed, revealing wooden struts to the merciless midday sun.

But strangely, perched on the top of one wall, was an oversized satellite dish: pristine, modern, and so out of place. Like the van, it seemed to purr, although satellite dishes don't do that, do they?

Scanning for strangers, I decided to inspect the scene a little more closely. Cautiously, I stepped forward, feeling curious, yet afraid. Noticing a brown smudge and a whimper, I realised that I was seeing a dog, soft and sleek, but straining on a leash tied to a steel pole.

Coming closer, I found I was holding my breath. It all felt wrong, very wrong, and all my senses heightened, like soldiers on alert.

A voice whispered hoarsely, inviting me to come closer.

I froze. Time seemed to slow down. It wasn't just the tone of the voice; it was the sensation that it was both coming from the dog, and inside my head at the same time. Without looking, I knew, I just knew, that there was no living person in the van, and no living person in the decaying house. There was only the staked out dog.
Reluctantly, I made eye contact. She stared back at me with green eyes. Dogs do not have green eyes, I knew. She stared at me with a look that may have been recognition. The hoarse whisper echoed more strongly in my skull this time.

Dogs can't smile, but this one seemed to curl the edges of its snout, like a leaf curls in a fire. It was unpleasant and threatening. I became more aware of the heat of the sun, and wondered if the glare was causing me to hallucinate the worrying grin. Was I imagining the voice and the clear, green eyes?

She held my eyes, and I walked across the parched earth. Almost hypnotized, I barely noticed the satellite dish begin to swivel, barely noticed the VW's engine turn off, barely noticed a hawk carving through the sky ahead. I walked towards the dog, and her fur seemed ever softer, and to take on a glossier shine.

But a memory startled me. Villagers used to stake out a goat, didn't they, to catch a tiger? A temptation, a trick, before the villagers sprang out in a blizzard of spears or arrows. What was I being lured to? [525 words]

How do I know this is a description, and not a story? Well, I make sure that very little happens – the narrator walks towards a VW van and thinks that a dog is talking to him or her.

Are you allowed to have brief events like this in your description? Well, look at the other question: "Or: Describe an occasion when you felt under confident or challenged. Write about your thoughts and feelings at that time."

This is exactly what I have just written above. My description would actually fit both questions. Does it matter that I have not written about my own real life challenge? No. I just have to be "inventive" and "compelling".

"Polygamy – the art of parrot-folding."
- Lizzy Mace

What does the examiner really want?

Here is another question 5 sample:

You are going to enter a creative writing competition.

Your entry will be judged by a panel of people of your own age. **Either**: Write a description suggested by this picture: Imagine a picture of a train, by a small, village, in a valley filled with snow.

Or: Write the opening part of a story about a place that is severely affected by the weather.

(24 marks for content and organisation 16 marks for technical accuracy, 40 marks)

Planning a point of view

Planning is essential in this question, even though it does not get marked. In the planning stage, you get to free up your thoughts. Apart from stopping you running out of ideas, this will also allow you to be original.

For example, what point of view might I write this description from?

- A passenger on the train
- A person in the town
- Someone stranded in their car
- The snow storm itself

Or, your choices might have been:
- The omniscient narrator
- A child on the train
- An evacuee from the city during a war
- An animal, looking at this view

When you look at these, I hope you can see that most ideas seem to flow naturally from the one before it. Again, that's what thinking looks like. I write down anything that comes into my head, and the act of thinking of an alternative tricks my brain into adapting or altering the original idea.

What I never do is sit there thinking, "what can I write, how shall I start?" These are just negative thoughts. Write down all your ideas, without saying no. Once you have done, it is simple to choose the idea that will be most interesting. Usually, the one that is most interesting for you to write will be the one that will be most interesting for the examiner to read. It is usually the third or fourth idea.

The third or fourth option will always give you an original answer that few other candidates, or no other candidates have thought of. This should always be the first part of your planning. Once you have a point of view, you will have an interesting perspective to look from. Because this narrows down your options, it will help you think and be creative.

The choices might also involve writing a full story. Avoid that choice unless you know you are brilliant at writing short stories. They require far more skill than writing a description or a chapter, because you need to know how they will end. You will learn what I mean by that as your read on.

Planning your description

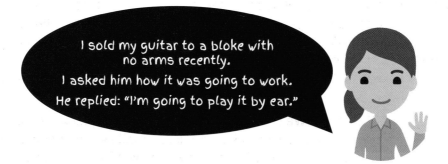

You don't actually need to refer much to the photograph (although you can). This is because the question is: "write a description *suggested* by this picture". There is no need for you to describe the actual picture. You can change as much of it as you like. The examiner only wants to see how good you are at writing a description.

I personally find this more helpful. In your revision, you need to practise different ways of using pictures. Take some from this guide, or at random from the internet. Try to write about them with this same question: "write a description suggested by this picture".

Now try it this way. Draw the picture in a few days' time. Include any details you like, that you know weren't' in the original picture. Give yourself a maximum of two minutes to do this. This will mean that your brain will not keep saying "no" to any of your ideas. At this stage, you want as many ideas as possible. It is a scribble, not a masterpiece. It will also help you to think visually.

- Whether with the photograph, or the drawing, you now need to label the things that interest you. Do this quickly in 30 seconds.

- Next, add in as many senses as you can. Concentrate on the ones most students won't think about. Start with touch. Include texture. This makes your writing figuratively feel three dimensional.

- Sound is a very important sense. In your planning stage, you never say no, you don't let your mind edit. For example, my first thought about the door was that it 'creaked'. Once I wrote this down, a better idea came to me, it 'groaned'. This was more unusual. When I came to write about it, I used it to write a simile. This came to me because I realized that groaned gave me the sound, but also the movement of a mouth opening, like a door opens. Then I asked myself what would groan from my character's point of view? My simile, 'like a teenager' tells my readers that the narrator is not a teenager.

- Now, all this happened because I didn't sit and think. When you sit and think, you weigh up your idea, and then reject it, and then wait for another idea, and then that might take a long time to come, and soon two minutes have gone by. Students genuinely believe this is thinking. But it isn't, it is editing and censorship, and it adds to your exam nerves. Worse than that, in those two minutes, you earned zero marks.

- Writing is thinking. As soon as you write down any old rubbish – "creaked", and then keep writing, your brain will automatically come up with more ideas. This only works if you never say no in the planning stage.

- Taste and smell are the next senses. These are very difficult to do well. Often students will add them in, because they are senses, but choose stereotypical sounds and smells. For example, "the whole place was dirty and smelled old." This could be improved, "the whole place was dirty, suffused with the smell of decay." This creates more of an image, not just old, but seedy or rotting, and "suffused" suggests the smell is everywhere, though not overpowering.

- But even better is if you can use the sense of smell in a metaphorical way. "The sky snapped into focus and smelled brightly of hope." Here the scene itself is vibrant. It is almost impossible for you not to have pictured a clear, blue sky, even though I have not said this is the case. That is because of the metaphor. Similarly, the smell of hope tells us precisely the mood of the character, which is optimistic and happy, even though we have described the sky. Because the smell is bright, we automatically assume it is a sunny day. Again, this is how metaphors work, and why they will make your descriptions brilliant.

- How do you get to this stage? Well, once you have labeled your picture with the senses, you ask yourself one question. "What is this like?" Again, you will get lots of ideas, often similes. Write them down, without saying "no". The act of writing will free up your thinking, and you will get new ideas. (In my example below, I wrote "growling" next to my dog. But then I realized this was predictable, and imagined it "whining". Then, because people whine, I had the idea of a talking dog, or at least a telepathic one, that could speak inside my character's head. Also, because the word "growling" was between the dog and the VW van in my picture, I suddenly wondered if the van could be "growling". This is how thinking works. Practise it. Practise not saying "no" to your ideas, and free up your thinking).

Five minutes of this and you are ready to go.

Summary of how to practice planning

- Draw on your picture, or recreate a new one based on the photograph.
- Label it with the senses, starting with texture and touch.
- Add an alternative for each, which will make you more original.
- Then sound and smell. Again, add alternatives.
- Ask what these words are "like" so that you think in similes and metaphors.

There are two skills that will influence the examiner:

- When you are writing a description, it is very easy to begin writing a narrative. Once your writing becomes a story, it stops keeping to its purpose. If it is not "consistently matched to purpose" it is unlikely to get more than 16 marks out of 24.

  To get 19 out of 24, your description needs to be "Convincingly matched to purpose", so even a bit of storytelling will make the examiner feel that you are not convincing. This is why, when I had a talking dog, I didn't actually use any direct speech. I don't want some idiot of an examiner thinking I can't write a description because one sentence in the whole piece is 'wrong'.

- The other skill is accurate punctuation. This is what the top grade demands: "Wide range of punctuation is used with a high level of accuracy." This is an issue, because different examiners will have different views about what it means.

  For example, what is a "wide range"? Does it mean that you have to include colons and semi-colons? What if your writing doesn't need a colon or semi-colon? It is quite possible that the examiner might ignore this fact, and simply penalise you for not having lots of different types.

  And what about commas and dashes? The same. Looking back at my example, I'm showing off my skills with commas, layering it with clauses and phrases. This might not be enough for a box ticking examiner, so I have had to make sure that I have at least a colon and a semi-colon. Real writers don't do this of course, but this is an exam, and your aim must always be to get 100%.

The solution is to practise using this kind of punctuation. The practice is artificial. However, this will mean that it comes more naturally to you in the exam.

Don't leave alphabet soup on the stove and go out: it could spell disaster.

Chapter 13: Learning How to Punctuate Like an Expert

(Again – this is not a hairdressers and the dog did not eat your revision – no short cuts, no excuses. Just do it.)

Colons:
These are used for three reasons.

1. To introduce an explanation.
   - Spectators stopped watching Formula One: changes to race rules meant that drivers stopped overtaking and races became more and more predictable.
   - Students complain about homework: boredom turns them into rebels.
   - Employers complain about the standard of English of school leavers: they can't spell and punctuate properly.
2. To introduce a list.
   - There are so many problems in the world: rampant pollution, middle eastern wars and daytime TV.
   - Miss Smith loved teaching her classes: the eager year 7s, the cynical year 9s, and even the comatose year 11s.
3. To introduce a quotation in a newspaper or magazine article.
   - Father Christmas has gone on strike. He says: "There are too many dangers to my reindeer, but the final straw was when the five year olds tried to pull off their noses."
   - One Direction have split. A spokesman for the band stated: "We were like, yeah, and then we were like, no, and y'know, the magic had, like, y'know, gone, and we all want to be Justin Bieber. Like, have you seen my tattoo?"

Note that this is the only time that the colon needs a capital letter after it.

4. To balance two contrasting ideas.
   - Children run in open spaces: their noses run in many places.
   - The way to a man's heart is through his stomach: it's quicker to use a knife though.
   - Summer comes on lazy tides: winter comes on furious winds.

Semi-colons
These are used for two reasons.

1. To separate longer items in a list.
   - I finally lost patience with the TV, fed up with the endless Bake-offs; the pointless game shows, full of hapless losers; endless re-runs of people trying to move house; soaps where all the characters SHOUT at each other, and anything with the words Ant or Dec.

2. To show that two sentences are related strongly to each other.

- He was late for their date; he found his car scratched when he returned.

- I felt exhausted by the time I got home; my wife brought me a cup of tea and a man-up pill.

- The dog had to be put down; he didn't even know he was cocky. (Think about it!)

Commas

What will most mark you out is your skill in controlling sentences that require commas.
The quickest way to do this is practice moving the subordinate clause around.

Example

- Having finished his homework, Mark celebrated by watching Bake Off.
- Having finished his homework, Mark celebrated by watching Bake Off, dreaming of a celebratory cake.
- Having finished his homework, Mark celebrated by watching Bake Off, dreaming of a celebratory cake, especially the coffee and praline masterpieces.
- Having finished his homework, Mark celebrated by watching Bake Off, dreaming of a celebratory cake - especially the coffee and praline masterpieces - while texting his lazy sister.
- Having finished his homework, Mark celebrated by watching Bake Off, dreaming of a celebratory cake - especially the coffee and praline masterpieces - while texting his lazy sister, to taunt her: she was still struggling with her art homework.

Example of how to move these around:

- Mark celebrated by watching Bake Off (having finished his homework), dreaming of a celebratory cake, especially the coffee and praline masterpieces, while texting his lazy sister, to taunt her: she was still struggling with her art homework.

- While texting his lazy sister, to taunt her, Mark celebrated by watching Bake Off (having finished his homework) and dreaming of a celebratory cake , especially the coffee and praline masterpieces: she was still struggling with her art homework.

- Having finished his homework, while texting his lazy sister, to taunt her (she was still struggling with her art homework), Mark celebrated by watching Bake Off, dreaming of a celebratory cake, especially the coffee and praline masterpieces

Why you should move the subordinate clauses around:

- Works by making Mark's celebration the most important detail.
- Works by making Mark's taunting of his sister the most important detail.
- Works by making the finishing of homework the most important detail.

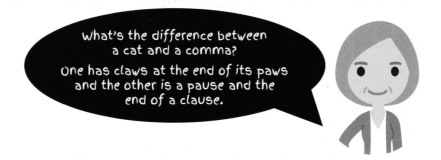

What's the difference between a cat and a comma?
One has claws at the end of its paws and the other is a pause and the end of a clause.

This shows you why it is worth moving the subordinate clause around, so that you emphasise the right information.

So, one way to get better at this technique is simply to practice it, adding a phrase or clause at a time.

Another way to practice this is to find a paragraph of another writer's text, and come up with a reason for each piece of punctuation. Then try to write something using the same punctuation, for the same reasons.

The Importance of Openings

There needs to be something unusual about your beginning. The easiest way to do this is start straight in with some action. This always forces the reader to ask questions: who is this, what is happening; why is it happening; where is it taking place; what is the time period; what is the genre?

When I say action, I mean taking place, not completed. Completed actions become stories, and stop being descriptions. Your action has to be continuous. In this case, the narrator is walking towards a dog, and the action largely takes place in the narrator's head. There aren't lots of events.

Start each sentence with a different word
You also need to be careful to practise starting each sentence with a different word.
My first four paragraphs contained sentences starting like this:

Something. The. It. Although. Yet. Standing. The. It's. One. Above. But. Like? Scanning. Cautiously. Noticing.

This happens automatically now, because I have practised it. I no longer have to think about this when I write. The good news for you, is that I only learned this as a teacher, showing my students how to write well. I haven't learned it because I have an English degree, but by practising it in class. You should do the same.

If you look at that list of words, you will also see a number of other advantages this gives my writing.

- Lots of words involve looking at things from a different perspective – although, yet, but and, because it starts a simile here, like.
- Starting sentences in this way also makes them longer and more detailed – good description does this.
- Several sentences start with verbs - standing, scanning, noticing. The participle ending (-ing) stops the actions being completed. This trick slows down time, and stops my description from having events that will turn it into a story.
- Starting a sentence with an adverb – cautiously – has the same effect of slowing down time.

How should I practice for this question?

The best way to practise openings is to find a really good book. Then imitate that writer. Here's how. My example comes from *A Darkling Plain*, by Philip Reeve.

Chapter one: Super – gnats over Zagwa

Because his book is still in copyright, I can't copy it. However, this is how the first paragraph is structured. I have kept all his punctuation and linking words.

Proper noun verb **since** noun; **first on the** adjective noun **and** noun **and** adjective noun **behind the** noun, **then** adverb noun **of** adjective noun, **and up at last onto the** adjective noun, verb **where** pronoun verb **to** noun and noun **where the** adjective noun verb. **The** noun **was** verb adverb **by the time** pronoun verb **the** noun. Pronoun verb **there a while to** verb noun **and** verb **his** noun. **Around him the** noun verb **behind** noun **of** noun verb **from the** noun **and** noun.

The bold words are ones I have kept the same as Reeve's book. Now, in order to learn to write brilliant openings, like a brilliant writer, I simply write my own story following his structure as precisely as I can. (I will expect to deviate slightly, but you get better at being exact through practice).

Jessica had been running **since** mid-day: initially along **the** crowded streets **and** avenues **and** alleys throughout **the** city, **then** across the parks **of** spreading suburbs, **and** outwards finally to scented meadows, watching **where** she could for starlings **and** swallows **where** her golden hopes flew. **The** sky **was** darkening above **by the time** she stopped at **the** wood. She waited **there a while to** drink in the greenness **and** finish her supplies. **Around her the** trees whispered **in** throngs **of** conspirators shouldering **up** the slopes **and** hills.

In bold, you can see where I have kept the same linking words. In highlighting is where I have had to add in a couple of extra linking words. But overall, Phillip Reeve is still teaching me how to write, so that my rhythms are just like his.

Of course, to do this, you really need to understand grammar. This is why we study grammar – it will make you a better writer. Learn it now.

The past, present and future walked into a bar. It was tense.

Practice number 2
The third paragraph of Philip Reeve's novel is structured like this:

Adverb adverb Proper noun verb **his way onto** a adjective noun **that** verb **down from the** adjective noun. **On either** noun **of him** adjective noun verb **for** adjective **of** noun **to a** noun **of** adjective noun; noun; adjective noun, verb, verb, adverb, **end over end, for ever. Ahead**, Proper noun **could** verb noun **but the** adjective noun. **He** verb adverb, verb a adjective noun, verb the adjective adjective noun **to the** noun **of the** noun, **and** verb.

I've just watched The Jungle Book, and I really like Baloo the bear. So, I am going to write something about him, using the structure above.

Eagerly, excitedly, Baloo made **his way up to** the golden cliff **that** taunted **him from its** impossible height. **On a** ledge **high above his** pathetic reach buzzed cocky swarms **of** bees **from** hive **to** hive **of** gourmet honey; treasure; golden bombs, calling, mocking, infuriatingly **out of reach, for ever. Up high**, Baloo could scoop honey **but not** from here. **He** sprinted suddenly, jumped **at the** ragged cliff, climbed **the** sharp impossible crags **of the** cliff, **and** prayed.

Reeve uses adverbs and adjectives to slow down the action. This works, because although there is one event – Baloo, trying to climb the cliff – the attempt is described in vivid detail through the use of adverbs and adjectives.

What might you learn as a writer from this paragraph.

- Starting a sentence with two adverbs is unusual, and dramatically slows time down.
- Writing long, convoluted sentences slows time down.
- Using two, three and sometimes four verbs in a sentence gives real action to the description, but if they are in one sentences, time is slowed down again.

Now, I have taught my students how to slow down time in their description for years. But the third bullet point is new to me. I just hadn't thought about it. However, Philip Reeve taught it to me just now, because I let him. I tried to copy the rhythm of his sentences. This is how you will learn best. Don't just read this guide, try the techniques. You know where to post them for me to comment.

Chapter 14: How to Write a Short Story as a Monologue

Just tell me what to do

- Think of something in the news from yesterday or today
- Start with the crisis
- Decide whose point of view will you write it from so that you can explore conflicting views
- Plan the best ending you can think of based on your character's point of view
- Start writing – points 6 to 12 will take care of themselves if you have practised them
- Remember to try to make each sentence start in a different way
- Show off with the best vocabulary you can think of
- Use adverbs, long clauses, verbs ending in '-ing' if you want to zoom in or slow down time
- Speed up time with short sentences or lots of verbs
- Show the reader, don't tell. Let the reader work things out
- Show off your descriptive techniques
- Play with punctuation
- Use all of the "showing off" skills from the descriptive writing advice above

(These cover all the skills of the mark scheme, as you will see below)

What does the question look like?

"Write the opening part of a story about a place that has spectacular scenery.
(24 marks for content and organisation 16 marks for technical accuracy) [40 marks]"
- (AQA specimen paper)

"Describe an occasion when you felt uncertain or unprepared. Focus on your thoughts and feelings at that time.
(24 marks for content and organisation 16 marks for technical accuracy) [40 marks]"
- (AQA specimen paper)

What does the mark scheme say?

AO5 Content and Organisation:
- Communicate clearly, effectively and imaginatively, selecting and adapting tone, style and register for different forms, purposes and audiences.
- Organise information and ideas, using structural and grammatical features to support coherence and cohesion of texts.

For 22-24 marks:

Assessment Objective 5:
Content
- • Register is convincing
- • Everything matches your purpose
- • Ambitious vocabulary with lots of linguistic devices

Assessment Objective 5:
Organisation
- • Inventive structural features
- • Convincing and complex ideas
- • Fluently-linked paragraphs

AO6 Technical Accuracy:
Candidates must use a range of vocabulary and sentence structures for clarity, purpose and effect, with accurate spelling and punctuation.

For 13 to 16 marks:
- • Sentence demarcation is consistently secure and consistently accurate
- • Wide range of punctuation is used with a high level of accuracy
- • Uses a full range of appropriate sentence forms for effect
- • Uses Standard English consistently and appropriately with secure control of complex grammatical structures
- • High level of accuracy in spelling, including ambitious vocabulary
- • Extensive and ambitious use of vocabulary

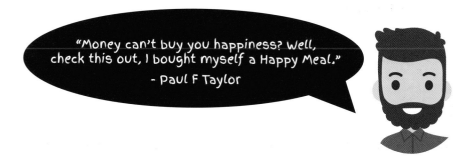

"Money can't buy you happiness? Well, check this out, I bought myself a Happy Meal."
- Paul F Taylor

Model answer 1

Question 5
Write a short story suggested by the picture on the following page.

(This could be the picture for the first option, the descriptive question. Now look again at one of the story questions above: "Describe an occasion when you felt unsure or challenged. Focus on the thoughts and feelings you had at that time." Because I am writing about a crisis that my character has, it will easily fit that question. But I got all my ideas from the photograph. You can do this too)

The face

I don't think you understand, do you? I mean, how could you, how could you possibly? I suppose, when you look at me, when you truly look at me, you don't really see what's there. That's the point. My eye, how it fixes you with an open stare, how it dares you to look away. You're not used to that, are you?

You remember me. Everyone remembers me. England's queen of starts, going on the b of bang. The gold medals, always the gold medals, and the impossible comebacks. 2020, 2024. I'm a legend, a national treasure, an inspiration. And of course the honours – Sports Personality of the Year, twice, Dame: Kathy Stringer, invincible, indomitable, incredible me.

Can you feel it? The roar of the crowd like a train rushing past you, threatening to carry you off your feet, to carry you to glory. Your name, chanted in two rhythmic syllables. Ka-thy, Ka-thy, Ka-thy by eighty thousand people, of all nationalities, of all ages, united, spellbound, as the clock shows another world record.

And I'm white. White girls don't run this fast. But I do. Oh, I really do.

And then of course, come the spin offs – the early mornings, looking wonderful on TV – I know you've watched me countless times on the cooking show spinoffs, the recipe books, and the Bake Off and Strictly. The heat of stardom – you can feel it can't you, like a bonfire; I light up like a beacon, like hope.

Because it isn't just about me. Sure, my clothes are pored over by the press, and my fashion label is a by-word for quality in gyms across the country. I am fitness. I am health. But look at all the girls, ready to give up sport in their early teens, who are inspired by me to try harder, to play a little longer. I fill the netball courts and the athletic tracks, and the lycra temples where girls crave fitter bodies, stronger bodies, better bodies. I did that. Girls becoming confident women, healthier women – women who will live longer, better lives. Yes, it isn't the added years to your life, it's the added life to your years. The secret ingredient – me, Kathy, girl-next-door Kathy, sporting legend Kathy, darling of the nation Kathy.

That's what you see.

But you don't see what I see. The mirror tells me the truth. Look more closely at my bottom lip, how it seems to sit on a ledge of flesh, cute, but slightly odd. It isn't there in the early photographs of me, but you haven't noticed. My gorgeous eyes, yes, "cobalt" in The Sun, "azure pools" in The Daily Mail – how often have you swum in their gaze as I advertise a world of health and beauty?

This is what you should see. One day soon, you will. My blood passport will be revoked. My borders will have been crossed. Gene therapy, new, wonderful and powerful, like an avalanche, wipes clean my muscles, pristine as fresh fallen snow. Muscles made more powerful, forged in a furnace of gene therapy. It won't be long now till the scientists catch up, till their tests on my stored blood samples will reveal the truth. I am not what I once was, but genetically enhanced. Genetically better.

Will I cower in the public gaze? Will I crave forgiveness from a deceived public? Will I beg to be accepted for what I truly am?

What do you think?   [574 words]

"I keep writing letters to myself. Dear me."
- Mark Simmons

The importance of planning the ending

This is difficult. I know that the ending is what students do worst. You remember that the mark scheme demands a crafted ending. But in the exam I have very little time to plan this. In normal story writing this is very difficult, because I will probably need lots of events to get me to the desired ending. But there is not enough time in the exam for loads of events.

Writing as my character, however, liberates me. I don't know how the story should end, but when I look at it through her eyes, it is easy. She will be found out. She won't regret a thing. She will remain defiant.

Then, I simply rely on the trick of repeating an idea from the beginning at the end: "What do you think?" The challenge for the reader is in deciding on her tone – is her emphasis on 'think', wanting the approval of the reader? Or is the emphasis on 'you', emphasising her contempt for the reader?

This isn't a cliff hanger, as the reader will jump one way or the other, towards a definite conclusion.

What does the examiner really want?

How have I tried to control the examiner?
- By writing a monologue from the character's viewpoint.
- By addressing the reader directly, as "you".
- By starting immediately with a challenge, a crisis.
- By starting mid-thought the character knows what she is talking about, but the reader really has to concentrate to try to catch up.
- By trying to give my character a voice. Her characteristics are repetition, contrast, vanity and pride. They didn't have to be, the picture just suggested that kind of character to me, so I went with it.
- You'll notice that having a monologue allows me to use some of the rhetorical techniques = contrasting pairs, repetition, emotive language. They all count.
- By crafting an ending that echoes the beginning, and forces the reader to fill in the blanks.

- By loading it up with similes and metaphors, because descriptive techniques still count.
- By loading up complex sentences in which I can show off my control of dashes, commas, colons and question marks.
- By interrupting the reader with short, one-sentence paragraphs.
- By having deliberately short sentences, for the same reason.

Try your own monologue and post it on my channel.

What do I have to do to get 100%?

Where do ideas come from? Ok, what is the source of the story about the athlete (The Face)? Well, I try to avoid films, as unimaginative students will rely on films. It is September, and the Olympics are only a month old, so they are on my mind. I have in mind Dafne Schippers, an extraordinary athlete, who became a sprinter late in her career, winning a 200m silver medal in Rio. In 2015, she beat all the world's top sprinters, and very unusually in sprinting, she is Dutch.

And in the news last week and this week are the medical details of athletes, stolen by Fancy Bears, the Russian backed hackers, who want revenge for being banned from the Olympics. Russian athletes were banned because of state-sponsored doping. The hackers also revealed some of our athletes take legal medicines when perhaps they don't need them, to enhance their performance. I ask myself, why would an athlete do that? Why would they do it, knowing that, at some point, science will catch up with their blood sample. Fame and glory can be bought, but will not last.

I don't know this is what I am going to write when I sit down and look at the picture. I just let my thoughts wander for a minute, and then begin writing. I wander over the photo. What catches my attention? It is the details that don't look quite right. The extra-large eye, the strange ridges below the bottom lip. I ask myself, what could have caused this?

I could have written about a woman who felt constantly judged for her appearance, but was so much more than this.

I could have written about an actress, who overcomes her looks to become a star, like Dame Judy Dench.

I could have written about a mother who stares defiantly at the camera, having killed her disabled child (something similar had happened in a book I have just finished reading).

I could have written about a woman who refuses to be judged on her looks, but demands to be taken seriously as a writer, or head teacher, or whatever.

My point is, if you wonder about the image, you will wonder about the details. Zoom in on them, and ask what they tell you about the person. You need to practise this. It is very easy to do. Pick any photograph in a newspaper. Or do it with real people, in a queue, in the street, on the bus. What is their story? What choices are they having to make?

This bit is crucial. Characters always make choices that are difficult, and that are different to the choices we make. This is how your story will come to life.

Start with their choice, and that will be your crisis.

All stories are like this. Little Red Riding Hood chooses to leave the path. The Three Little Pigs choose to make houses quickly but cheaply. Jack and the Beanstalk, choosing to sell the cow for magic beans. Cinderella, choosing to flee the ball before her real identity is uncovered. Once you have your character, you have their choice, and you have your crisis.

Pick your stories from life, not film or TV

My next choice, as a writer in the exam, is to think differently to everyone else. I know I will be different because I have based my story on my observations of real life, rather than copied a film, TV series, or a book. I am willing to settle for an idea inspired by a book – after all, a very good writer will have given me the idea, writers know how to write stories, but I will be more original working from life.

I've also stolen words that I've heard this weekend – the one about 'not the extra years on your life, but the extra life in your years'. I heard on TV, in response to Mark Zuckerberg's announcement this week, that he wanted to eradicate disease. 'It's not about me' is a line in the book I just finished reading a couple of hours ago. 'The B of Bang' was a phrase used by Linford Christie, a famous British sprinter and drug cheat when I was younger.

In other words, be alert to the world around you. The world is shoving information at you all the time. Let it in – then you won't have to go looking for it. Stories will just come to you.

How do you get ideas from the news?

The news is full of stories. For you, it might be easier to pay attention to your family. There will be many stories right there – but you may be too close to them to see them for what they are. So take a look at the news.

Here is some stuff from the papers just today:
- Kim Kardashian has been robbed by highly intelligent and effective jewel thieves. They monitored her Facebook, Twitter and Instagram accounts, worked out when she would be in her hotel, bound the hotel concierge, tied her up and robbed her of millions of dollars of jewellery. How did they escape? By bicycle. Imagine writing the story from the point of view of the youngest member of the gang. Or you could write it unsympathetically about Kim Kardashian – Graham Norton's joke was, Kim was asked if she thought it was an 'inside job', and she replied, "what's a job?" Or you could write it from her point of view – staging the whole thing to keep her name in the headlines.
- Or Donald Trump, presidential nominee in America. A ten-year-old video of him and the president's son, Billy Bush, has just been released, in which Trump boasts of grabbing women's privates, forcing kisses on them: "when you're a star, they let you do it. You can do anything." Total sexism. Very easy for you to write a story in which he loses the election to a woman – Hilary Clinton. Of course, you might know nothing about politics – you could translate this as a story involving the most popular boy in Year 11, and how he gets revealed as sexist by the girls he has abused with "banter".

- Or you could write it from the point of view of the soap star who greets Donald and Billy. Her name is Arianna Zucker. What revenge might she have planned? Here's the actual transcript.

  Zucker: Are you ready to be a soap star?
  Trump: We're ready, let's go. Make me a soap star.
  Bush: How about a little hug for Donald? He just got off the bus?
  Zucker: Would you like a little hug, darling?
  Trump: Okay, absolutely. Melania (Trump's wife) said this was okay.
  Bush: How about a little hug for the Bushy? I just got off the bus.
  Zucker: Bushy, Bushy.

  What might she do to them on the set of the Soap? What if they made it a live recording? What if she recorded this conversation, and stored it for just the right moment?

- Two UKIP members of the European parliament were involved in a fight, after which one collapsed and spent days in hospital. One was called Mr Woolfe, who got blown down, and the other Mr Hookem! What if all political debate were carried out through boxing, or mixed martial arts? What if each party had to nominate a champion MP to fight for them where the party could not agree on a policy – for example whether we should let in more refugees? Whether we should have more grammar schools?

- In California, a concert was held with the most famous old rock stars: Mick Jagger and the Rolling Stones, Paul McCartney, Bob Dylan, Roger Waters and The Who, in a production costing over $100 million. The average age of the rock stars was 72. What if one of them died on stage with a heart attack? What if they formed a secret group who controlled the world – brainwashing the rich audience of 50 and 60 somethings who control all the wealth in America and the UK? What if they turn out to be aliens, and the musical gathering was a cover for a signal to their mother ship, that would come to transport them home?

- A greater percentage of female soldiers are fitter than male soldiers. Women soldiers are also now allowed to fight on the front line. What would an army look like in which the best soldiers were women? Would they be more caring peace keepers, or would they be more daring and violent? What kind of story could I put them in? A female soldier rescuing her colleagues under fire in a warzone? A fight between a female soldier and a sexist male officer? A teenager fighting her mother's desire for her to become a doctor, and choosing to join the army.

- The pound dropped in value by 6% in four minutes of trading this week because traders were using a computer programme that reads the news, and judges whether reactions to Brexit are positive or negative. It had counted too many negative stories, and told all its offices to sell pounds and buy dollars. What would you do if you could control the computer programme – would you cost the country billions, if it meant you could earn those billions? What if the computer programme took control itself – how would you stop it before it devalued the pound too far and sold the country to the highest bidder?

- Archaeologists have just uncovered the tooth of a 7000-year-old hunting dog that walked with hunters near Stonehenge. What if we didn't train dogs to be domesticated, but they instead trained us so that they no longer had to hunt? What if this was the first dog to do so? What if it persuaded human kind to stop hunting and settle down as farmers, feeding it and its descendants forever? What if we told the story through the dog's eyes?

You get the idea, stories are everywhere. All you have to do is keep your eyes open.

A psychologist is making a fortune selling a book to find out your dog's IQ. It costs £20. Here's how it works. If you buy the book, the dog's cleverer than you are.

Model answer number 2

Just tell me what to do

- Turn the question to your advantage by using an object or place to access memories, thoughts and feelings
- If you are given a photograph, include it in your beginning somehow, and then write what you want
- Use your childhood as a way into the question
- Plan an ending
- Start writing

Alternatively, base your story on your childhood

This particular idea was given to me by a children's author, Laura Dockrill, (http://www.lauradockrill.co.uk) which is how we know it will be a good one. She asked us all to imagine our first bedroom. You should try it. Here's what I wrote:

Dear Bedroom,

It's been a long time, hasn't it? Perhaps you remember me, as little as I remember you. You were literally another country. Is it Spanish now you speak, or another tongue?

Do you remember the cowboy fort? What did I do there? Jacey was there, we had a bunk bed. But I don't remember what we did. We had the wide, wide world, miles and miles across. Roaming. And the sea, not foaming, but calm. A whole other world we took to without fear. Yes, a childhood, free and unafraid. Is it different now?

You were windowless, a fact which now I find impossible to believe, like being blind. Perhaps that was my parents' genius, making the inside so prison like, (with its bunk beds and plain white walls) that we fled outside. Adventure. Health. Derring-do. Remember when the roof crashed in as we sped across it, and we clung to electric cables tied to the wall, while a thousand bottles in the bar's store room splintered below, and gaped like sharks' teeth?

Do you remember our dogs who had to be put down? They were so dumb, they'd claw each door until the right occupant opened, on the second floor, four doors away. Mum killed them rather than train them. She felt the loss terribly, but not as heavily as we did. A world without light and windows. I didn't blame her, nor feel guilt for the bar owner, just the unspeakable relief that we were still alive. Selfish and unquestioning, like survivors of a natural disaster.

And then the bankruptcy, and fleeing at dawn. You were suddenly empty. The new owners, what were they like? Did they drop bombs from the balcony at the unsuspecting tourists below, a blitzkrieg of origami and water? Did they run out on school days, without eating, saving their appetite for the chocolate sandwich on the way? Do the adults still return at 4am, when the bars are shut? Does the kitchen still sizzle to the sound of live crabs, just caught, being grilled on the 'plancha'?

I imagine now your flat is full of rebellious pensioners, determined to chase the sun in their final days. Raging against the dying light, they freeze vodka in their ice cubes so that their party guests get quickly drunk, like teenagers downing cider in the park. They are European now, a united nations of those who have left conformity behind: a travelling band, killing off the zombies of roast dinners, endless TV soaps, Jeremy flipping Kyle, talent(less) shows and pimp my property shows. They don't need windows when the real life's outside.

Much love,
Mr Salles   [444 words]

Here it is again for you to test yourself on the use of descriptive techniques in **SOAPAIMS** (I am a bit of a cheat, by the way, as they are all imagery).

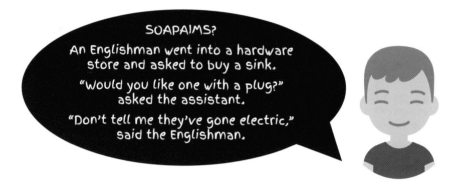

SOAPAIMS?

An Englishman went into a hardware store and asked to buy a sink.

"Would you like one with a plug?" asked the assistant.

"Don't tell me they've gone electric," said the Englishman.

Dear Bedroom 1,

It's been a long time, hasn't it? Perhaps you remember me, as little as I remember you. You were literally another country. Is it Spanish now you speak, or another tongue 2?

Do you remember the cowboy fort? What did I do there? Jacey was there, we had a bunk bed 3. But I don't remember what we did. We had the wide, 4 wide world 5, miles and miles across. Roaming. And the sea, not foaming 7, but calm. A whole other world 6 we took to without fear. Yes, a childhood, free 8 and unafraid. Is it different now?

You were windowless, a fact which now I find impossible to believe, like being blind 9. Perhaps that was my parents' genius, making the inside so prison like, (with its bunk beds and plain white walls) that we fled outside. Adventure. Health. Derring-do. Remember when the roof crashed in as we sped across it, and we clung to electric cables tied to the wall, while a thousand bottles in the bar's 10 store room splintered 11 below, and gaped like sharks' teeth? 12

Do you remember our dogs who had to be put down? They were so dumb, they'd claw each door until the right occupant opened, on the second floor, four 13 doors away. Mum killed them rather than train them. She felt the loss terribly, but not as heavily as we did. A world without light and windows.14 I didn't blame her, nor feel guilt for the bar owner, just the unspeakable relief that we were still alive. Selfish 15 and unquestioning, like survivors of a natural disaster.16

And then the bankruptcy, and fleeing at dawn. You were suddenly empty. The new owners, what were they like? Did they drop bombs from the balcony at the unsuspecting tourists below, a blitzkrieg of origami 17 and water? Did they run out on school days, without eating, saving their appetite for the chocolate sandwich on the way? Do the adults still return at 4am, when the bars are shut? Does the kitchen still sizzle 18 to the sound of live crabs, just caught, 19 being grilled on the 'plancha'?

I imagine now your flat 20 is full 21 of rebellious pensioners, determined to chase the sun 22 in their final days. Raging against the dying light 23, they freeze vodka in their ice cubes so that their party guests get quickly drunk, like teenagers downing cider in the park.24 They are European now, a united nations 25 of those who have left conformity behind: a travelling band, killing off the zombies 26 of roast dinners, endless TV soaps, Jeremy flipping Kyle, talent(less) shows and pimp my property 27 shows.

They don't need windows when the real life's outside.
Much love,
Mr Salles

Answers:

1P	8A	15A	22M
2A	9S	16S	23P
3A	10A	17M	24S
4A	11A	18O	25M
5M	12S	19A	26M
6M	13A	20P	27A
7O	14M	21A	

What do I have to do to get 100%?

Breaking the vase

Now, before I go through the descriptive skills, let me tell you about Philip Pullman, a brilliant author, who used to be a teacher. (http://www.philip-pullman.com). So there he was at Swindon's literature festival, and the audience full of readers, and you can imagine a fair few teachers. We all loved what he had to say about loving writing, being creative, having something worth saying. "But," asked a primary school teacher, "how can I allow my children to be creative, when at the end of the year they have to sit a SATs paper, with a title they have to write about, no matter how boring?"

Philip Pullman's reply was genius, and I have used it ever since. "Imagine," he said, "the most boring title in the world. *The Vase.* This is what you teach your creative child to do.

The boy strode into the room, picked up the vase, and smashed it against the wall.
"Now," he said, "you can write whatever you want."

So, let's imagine a picture of a train, or a road, or a park, or some other boring photo that means nothing to you in the exam. But, this morning, you just happen to be thinking about your childhood. And you want to write about that. Well, now you can.

"I've lost seven pounds this week. Or, as my girlfriend calls it, 'the baby'."
- Maff Brown

Here's how mine might start if the photograph were of a train:

"Dear Bedroom,

It's been a long time, hasn't it? Perhaps you remember me, as little as I remember you. You were literally another country, more than a train journey away; many stations have separated us, more with each passing year. Is it Spanish now you speak, or another tongue?"

Or imagine it was the park.

"Dear Bedroom,

It's been a long time, hasn't it? Perhaps you remember me, as little as I remember you. You were literally another country. Is it Spanish now you speak, or another tongue? Is the park still dark outside, full of white, chalky turds the Spaniards let their dogs leave behind?"

Or, the ultimate vase breaking, you can simply have it as the photo in the room. Imagine a photo of a road.

"Dear Bedroom,

It's been a long time, hasn't it? Does the bizarre picture of the road still hang where my mother left it? How I hated it. Perhaps you remember me, as little as I remember you. You were literally another country. Is it Spanish now you speak, or another tongue?"

So, now you have seen how you can be as creative as you like, let's look at the advantages of writing to your bedroom. This is just a way of writing about your childhood, by the way, it didn't have to be your bedroom. The point was to think creatively, and this is why we were asked to write it as a letter. Even more creative, we were asked to write to a noun, an object, something that would transport our minds in time and space, like a Harry Potter portal key.

Therefore, it could have been a letter to your favourite toy, your first bicycle, the park you played in... you get the idea: anywhere that would spark memories and feelings.

Let's look at some descriptive skills – there are plenty of them that make each paragraph original, but I will try to confine myself to three to tell you about in each paragraph. Feel free to spot more of your own, and use them in your writing.

What does the examiner really want?

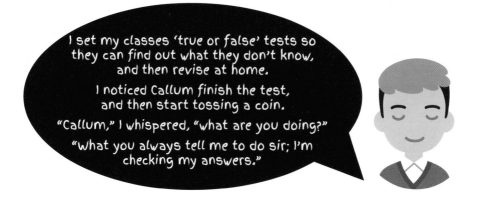

I set my classes 'true or false' tests so they can find out what they don't know, and then revise at home.
I noticed Callum finish the test, and then start tossing a coin.
"Callum," I whispered, "what are you doing?"
"What you always tell me to do sir; I'm checking my answers."

A look at descriptive techniques and interesting writing (More Than Just SOAPAIMS)

Dear Bedroom,

It's been a long time, hasn't it? Perhaps you remember me, as little as I remember you. You were literally another country. Is it Spanish now you speak, or another tongue?

- **It starts by addressing an inanimate object as though it were human.**
- **Rhetorical question.**
- **Use of contrast (then and now, English and foreign)**

Do you remember the cowboy fort? What did I do there? Jacey was there, we had a bunk bed. But I don't remember what we did. We had the wide, wide world, miles and miles across. Roaming. And the sea, not foaming, but calm. A whole other world we took to without fear. Yes, a childhood, free and unafraid. Is it different now?

- **The description of the place also introduces people.**
- **Deliberate use of repetition for emphasis.**
- **Deliberate use of alliteration and internal rhyme, to make the words memorable**.

You were windowless, a fact which now I find impossible to believe, like being blind. Perhaps that was my parents' genius, making the inside so prison like (with its bunk beds and plain white walls) that we fled outside. Adventure. Health. Derring-do. Remember when the roof crashed in as we sped across it, and we clung to electric cables tied to the wall, while a thousand bottles in the bar's store room splintered below, and gaped like sharks' teeth?

- **Similes**
- **Introduction of another perspective (my parents).**
- **Curtailed sentences (where they are not real sentences as they have no verbs) to provide drama (which has to fit the dramatic subject matter).**

Do you remember our dogs who had to be put down? They were so dumb, they'd claw each door until the right occupant opened, on the second floor, four doors away. Mum killed them rather than train them. She felt the loss terribly, but not as heavily as we did. A world without light and windows. I didn't blame her, nor feel guilt for the bar owner, just the unspeakable relief that we were still alive. Selfish and unquestioning, like survivors of a natural disaster.

- **A brief anecdote (a little incident that helps you picture a character – here my mother)**
- **Simile and metaphor.**
- **Deliberate use of contrast again.**

And then the bankruptcy, and fleeing at dawn. You were suddenly empty. The new owners, what were they like? Did they drop bombs from the balcony at the unsuspecting tourists below, a blitzkrieg of origami and water? Did they run out on school days, without eating, saving their appetite for the chocolate sandwich on the way? Do the adults still return at 4am, when the bars are shut? Does the kitchen still sizzle to the sound of live crabs, just caught, being grilled on the 'plancha'?

- **Direct questions**
- **Metaphor**
- **Anecdote**

I imagine now your flat is full of rebellious pensioners, determined to chase the sun in their final days. Raging against the dying light, they freeze vodka in their ice cubes so that their party guests get quickly drunk, like teenagers downing cider in the park. They are European now, a united nations of those who have left conformity behind: a travelling band, killing off the zombies of roast dinners, endless TV soaps, Jeremy flipping Kyle, talent(less) shows and pimp my property shows.

- **Metaphor and simile**
- **Anecdote**
- **Alliteration**

They don't need windows when the real life's outside.

Much love,

Mr Salles

- **An ending that refers back to an idea introduced near the beginning**
- **Metaphor**
- **Contrast**

I simply based this on my childhood: these were the images that came to me as I considered my bedroom. This forces my memories to have a shape. If I had just written about my childhood, growing up in Ibiza, I would have written about the outdoors. In fact, none of the details above would have made the cut; I have dozens of memories that are more interesting, as I am sure do you.

But, how would I decide which memories to include? How would I decide which order to put them in? How would I work out how to end it? This is the problem with most creative writing, we just don't know where to start and how to get to an ending.

However, Laura Dockrill saves us from this uncertainty, this avalanche of choice. She says, just focus on one thing, and trust that everything will flow from that. And we should trust her, she is a writer, and moreover her favourite author is Roald Dahl. Double trust.

My parents said they had to make a lot of sacrifices to pay for my education... I wondered where my pets had been going.

How to write a story based on your childhood

Just as with description, a story is best if you focus on only one thing. The thing that must always be at the forefront of your thinking is the ending. Endings make stories in the same way that flavour makes a meal. Otherwise, you are just chucking lots of ingredients together and hoping for the best.

If we look back at my descriptions, there are two possible endings – those moments when things finish. One is when we went bankrupt and lost everything, including the flat. The other is when my dogs were put down.

I can begin writing with both or either of those in mind. Here is the same description, now written as a story. Because I have the dogs' death in mind, I can just focus on this moment, the moment when the boy realises not just that death is real, but that his mother has chosen to kill. That's a pretty dramatic ending right there.

However, because my mother has now also died, in my mind, her death is also linked to the death of our dogs. I'll choose to combine these deaths. But don't read it and think, well, thanks Mr Salles, I can't do that, I've only been around for 16 years. That's ok; you'll go for my earlier ending.

Dear Bedroom,

Two years after my mother died, I think of you. When did childhood end? Was it when I gave the eulogy, told the impossible, hilarious, tragic, extraordinary life she had? There were earlier endings. At five, my grandmother died, and I didn't speak for a week. You remember me then, in the womb of your white walls, weeping, kicking against the sides, against the tides, against death.

It's been a long time, hasn't it? Leaving Spain was another death – when dad left, and mum started dating the bank robber, and the dream of Disneyland died, our savings taking us only as far as Canada – right continent, wrong country.

I didn't say goodbye, or send you a postcard from the border, leaving the sun and crossing into the snows. Nor a photograph, a snapshot of me ballooning to eleven stone: ten years old, and a giant snowball of a kid, out of place. Yes, that was a kind of ending, but really, I think the damage was already done, further back, when you still knew me.

We had the wide, wide world, miles and miles across. Roaming. And the sea, not foaming, but calm. A whole other world we took to without fear. Adventure. Health. Derring do. Remember when the roof crashed in as we sped across it, and we clung to electric cables tied to the wall, while a thousand bottles in the bar's store room splintered below, and gaped like sharks' teeth?

But do you remember when the dogs were put down? They were so dumb, they'd claw each door until the right occupant opened, on the second floor, four doors away. Mum drove them to the ends of the earth, unsuspecting in the back seat of the car. But Ibiza was small, and the earth ended only 25 miles away.

Fred smelt his way back, tracked us like an Indian scout, his happiness matched by mum's distress. Mum killed them rather than train them. She met us on the road from school, so the empty flat wouldn't swallow us up. She meant to spare us the goodbye, so they were killed while we weren't looking.

She felt the loss terribly, but not as heavily as we did. I didn't blame her. Selfish and unquestioning, like survivors of a natural disaster, we clung on to our childhoods then. We tried to rewrite the world. When I looked back, it was the fun and freedom I remembered. Dropping bombs from the balcony on the unsuspecting tourists below, a blitzkrieg of origami and water. Rushing out on school days, without eating, savouring the chocolate sandwich on the way.

I imagine now your flat is full of rebellious pensioners, determined to chase the sun in their final days. Raging against the dying light, they freeze vodka in their ice cubes so that their party guests get quickly drunk, like teenagers downing cider in the park. Life, joyful, refusing to give in. That's the way mum died in the end, staring death in the eye. The ward sister rang, while I was still two hours away. Hurry, she said. Your mother wants to say goodbye.

We got it right this time.

Much love,
Mr Salles   [534 words]

Just tell me what to do

- Pick a story from the news
- Think of a source of conflict
- Decide on which point of view write in order to explore that conflict
- Plan an ending that resolves the conflict
- Start straight in with the conflict and make the reader catch up with you

Model answer number 3: writing from the news

The Swindle

Kanye was exhausted. Another night shepherding the most photographed woman in the world around the Paris nightlife. Nothing was private. No trips to the patisserie or the boulangerie, no casual stroll to the Eiffel tower, no romantic walk along the Seine. **No, treats were ordered in; the atmosphere was artificial and air conditioned, in SUVs with blacked out windows**. Even the Lamborghini involved endless goes at the outfits, each one posed and carefully styled for Instagram, before he could even turn the engine on. **Tanya, the make-up artist, and Tony, the very camp dresser, would be called for 20 minutes before** the photographs, taken with professional lighting and made to feel authentic by the hand held iPhone, limited edition – a diamond encrusted gift from Apple. Priceless. Like the jewellery – diamonds from Tiffany's.

Yes, the rich got richer. Everything Kim touched turned to gold, or platinum, or diamond. Always in the headlines, always in the press, but much more importantly, always on social media – Snapchat, Instagram, Facebook, WhatsApp – she might just as well have invented them all. She played them all, like a grand master, moving pieces around countless boards, seeing patterns and moves that took him days to catch on to. She made sure the paparazzi were everywhere, and where they weren't, her social media stepped in like a presidential campaign; everything and anything to keep Kim in the news.

So, it had been another night club, another night of impossibly expensive champagne – Chateaux this, Don that. Kanye marvelled at how caviar had lost its flavour, how the exquisite bubbles of champagne felt flat the moment they met his tongue. He shut his eyes and sat back in the chair – the only furniture in their suite that felt real and not manufactured for tasteless millionaires. He tried to remember the feeling, before Kim, when he used to love music. He made music, and his music made headlines. Kanye and Kim. That's how it began. But now, it was Kim and Kanye. No, it was Kim, Kardashian and Kanye.

He remembered when he first heard Kardashian as a name. He had thought they were evil aliens in a Star Trek movie. With his eyes closed he could hear Kim next door, dropping millions of pounds worth of diamonds on the glass dresser. Then he imagined the faint clicks of the safe, before the jewellery rattled the table tops with the warning hiss of a rattle snake, before being silenced by the kiss of the closing steel door.

A sixth sense caused him to suddenly start. Time moved in slow motion. The sound of a card swipe at the lock, the handle turning; the grunt as he sprang forward, pushing hard on the arms of his chair; the door swinging open; a glimpse of two masked figures charging through; his lunge for the brass lamp; two more figures, dressed entirely in black, a sinister background to the first two: the inevitable realisation that they would overpower him...

He reached the lamp anyway, even had a hand on it, when the first figure made eye contact with him, holding between them a silver colt, gleaming and beautiful, and very definitely loaded. Kanye opened his mouth to warn Kim, but the second figure was already slamming a black hood over his head. His last image was of two lean and wiry shadows bursting through her bedroom door. Strong hands thrust him down, and the pounding of his own heart frightened him. He fought the terrible feelings of powerlessness and fear.

It can't have lasted more than a minute. His ears listened desperately to hear what might be happening next door. He fought down each fear, tried not to think the worst. He heard footsteps, no words. A harsh male laugh, but where he expected a scream from Kim, he was sure he heard her laugh. Impossible.

Hands suddenly left him, and he stumbled to her door, ripping the hood from his dazed eyes, not realising his feet were bound, until too late. Darkness.

He came to, and crawled to the doorway, "Kim! Kim!" he yelled, and fell through the door. The safe gaped open, like a mouth with each of its pearled teeth missing. Not a gem was left.

Kim sat, bound on the bed, her eyes bright with triumph. One eyebrow arched, daring him to think. [723 words.]

This is an easy length for me to reach in my 45 minutes. You will probably write more slowly, so I have got rid of all the words in bold – reread it without these words, and it will make perfect sense [543 words.]

What does the examiner really want?

The examiner is thinking this:
"For God's sake, give me something interesting to read, something I haven't read a dozen times before. A story with a proper ending. Just once, I'd like to read something in which no one gets killed. Why do teenagers keep slaughtering people? And no dreams, no flipping cliffhangers, pretending to be endings.

No more pointless dialogue to tell the story. And what is wrong with paragraphing – do you think you only get so many goes, and you are scared of using them all up?

Would it be too much not to start each sentence with "he, she, it, then, the" – stop boring me. Am I getting paid enough to read this stuff? I'm not sure I will mark again next year.
I can't read this hand writing! This is your GCSE.

When I start reading a simile it would be wonderful if I can't guess exactly how it is going to end – hmm, I wonder what it was as fast as? A cheetah perhaps, a racing car...what about as fast as hate, as slow as forgiveness, as quiet as dawn?

Why are you basing this on a film – they take two hours to watch and you only have 500 words – what are you, an idiot?

But what the examiner wants is this:

Ooh, this is interesting, I haven't seen this before. I really hope this keeps going, it would be such a relief to give an A* [the examiner will still be thinking in old grades].

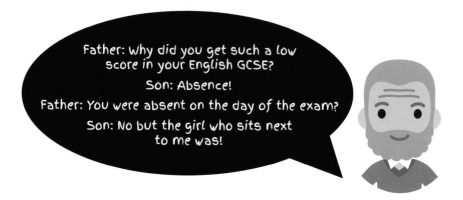

Father: Why did you get such a low score in your English GCSE?

Son: Absence!

Father: You were absent on the day of the exam?

Son: No but the girl who sits next to me was!

How can this teach you to write stories?

Ok, you know my starting point was simply something in the news.

The next, and most important skill, is in deciding on an ending. I really liked the twist where Kim Kardashian turns out to have planned the whole robbery herself. I had originally imagined writing it from her point of view. But then I realized this would not provide enough conflict, so I moved my narrator to her husband Kanye. My first idea was to set this up with a radio conversation between the thieves and their behind the scenes leader. I would make sure the voice was synthesised, to disguise it. This would lay the ground for my twist when it turns out to be Kim's voice, so that even the gang don't know that she is the leader behind the heist. Then Kanye would come into the room at the end, just as Kim is hiding her radio.

I was pretty pleased with this. However, this would cause me to split the action into two places – Kim talking to the gang, and then the separate robbery. The more scenes you have, the more words you need, the less likely to get it done inside 45 minutes. I haven't tried to write a short story in this time limit since I took my O level English language in 1980. In other words, I didn't need to be an English teacher to know that adding extra scenes would cost me too many words and too much time. You can know this too. I just needed to think like a writer. You should do the same.

So, I changed the ending so that Kanye still discovers it is his wife who has orchestrated the whole robbery. Without the exposition, where the gang receive instructions from a synthesised voice, how would I prepare the twist? For the ending to work, the reader has to think, "ah, so that's why you wrote such and such earlier on."

This actually improved my story, as I had to think much harder about the clues I was going to drop. This is only possible if you plan the ending first. Indeed, the ending is the only bit you need to plan. Once that is firmly in your mind, you will find you think on your feet as you write.

As I was writing, I also realized that the conflict in Kanye's perspective of his wife and their lifestyle was quite interesting. Here I do have the advantage of being married – it is amazing but also totally normal for spouses to have very different interpretations of the same events. This allowed me to create an ending in which Kim's sense of triumph could be caused by her refusing to be a victim and working out how to use this robbery for publicity. In this reading, she has been genuinely robbed. It is then only Kanye's perspective that suggests he suspects her. This ambiguity forces the reader to think hard about the story and notice the clues I have planted. This is the definition of "crafting" – the reader has to notice how I have structured it.

Let's look at the clues that I planted, to suggest that Kim was the mastermind. You will find them in my thought process below:

Think like a writer

1. **Show a motive – but do not tell the reader this.**

   The first paragraph links her jewellery to the desire for publicity through social media. This gives her a motive.

2. **Show your main character through the eyes of a different narrator. This forces the reader to have to infer, and forces you to drop clues.**

   The second paragraph links her control of social media to a highly intelligent plan, like a grand master at chess, and like a highly rehearsed political campaign for president. It also reveals that Kanye works things out eventually – this is important, because he needs to work out what has happened at the end, just as we do.

3. **Develop the viewpoint of your narrator.**

   The third paragraph makes sure that my narrator has a reason to notice things. He is my most important character, because if he doesn't notice, Kim keeps her secret, and there is no twist. The last line of the paragraph suggests that Kim is ruthless, so that the twist will also seem in character.

4. **Use description only to advance the plot.**

   Here it will help us realise she is behind the robbery. The description of the jewellery does not focus on its beauty. Instead, the simile to describe the diamonds, and sinister sibilance describing the safe, which mimics the hiss of the snake, suggests that the jewellery is dangerous. This plants the seed of the idea that Kim uses them as a weapon to draw out the gang and feed her need for publicity.

5. **Slow time down for the action, by focusing on tiny details and brief moments.**

   The next two paragraphs introduce the action and the crisis. Here it was necessary to keep Kim plausibly out of the room, so it had to happen quickly. Paradoxically, a great way to show actions happening quickly is to slow time down, focusing on individual moments, which you wouldn't notice when events play out in real time. Here I am helped by the long list of events happening both in sequence and simultaneously. As a stylistic choice, I could have written this scene with very short, punchy sentences, with one action coming quickly after another.

This would work but because I wanted the gang's actions to be described at the same time as Kanye's, drawing out these long sentences helps me juxtapose their actions. A further advantage is that it builds up my narrator's perspective; these long, convoluted sentences help us see his thoughts and feelings.

6. **Show the thoughts and feelings of your character or narrator to make the reader sympathise with them.**

As his thoughts keep turning to Kim, and keeping her safe, I build greater sympathy for him. However, I mainly do it to give my twist more power – her manipulation of the media will seem much less of a betrayal than her manipulation of him. For this reason, I also have a loaded gun pointed at his face, so that we can see that even though Kim has planned the robbery, she cannot have been sure that the gang would not have killed her husband. Yet her thirst for publicity was so great she was willing to take that risk.

I labour this point by having him fall and knock himself out as he tries to reach her. This increases our sense of his love for her, and so magnifies her betrayal. If I had simply had the gang club him, I would be painting Kim as too inhuman for my story – I don't want the reader to see her as a Lady Macbeth villain, willing to justify murder.

7. **Choose an ending that makes the reader infer. Do this with 'show, don't tell'.**

The ending, in which we infer that she has planned this all along, comes entirely from advice given to writers and by writers at every opportunity. Show, don't tell. This is what "show, don't tell" means. Of course, it also means all my other points above – each clue is a show, not a tell – I never tell you the significance of any of the clues, so that they only make sense at the end. Here, at the ending, the reader has to ask themselves why she is so triumphant, and why she is daring her husband to think. I added that last sentence to show that she expects her husband to be proud of her, and proud for himself when he works out the detail of her plot. I've done this because I want the reader to look again at the marriage and wonder just what is it that keeps Kim and Kanye together.

8. **Kill Your Babies**

You should also have noticed all the things I left out of this story. I deliberately chose Kim and Kanye because I know almost nothing about them – I know that Kim has sisters, that her father got OJ Simpson acquitted of a murder he almost definitely committed, and that she is famous for selfies of her improbably large bottom. Kanye is a singer and that she has dark hair. If you showed me a photograph of either of them, I would have no idea who they are. This helped me a great deal, because it meant I would not waste time describing them because many of my readers would spot mistakes in my descriptions but, more importantly, because description slows down the story. I only use description if it is going to help suggest the characters' thoughts and feelings, or if it will prepare for my plot twist.

I knew a deal more about the gang – that they come from eastern Europe, probably Montenegro. That they have carried out a string of multi-million pound jewel robberies, that the pieces are likely to have been stolen to order, not to be cut up and sold as individual diamonds; that they get fake identities for the stolen diamonds, showing them as coming from war-torn countries like Sierra Leone; that they are always armed, but have never fired a shot, and finally the rather brilliant detail that they made their escape by bicycle. I was desperate to include this last detail, but it would have ruined the impact of the twist of my ending. Writers call this "killing your babies". Your favourite things might not fit your story. And everything, absolutely everything, has to fit your story. Those are the rules and to work out how everything fits, you start with the ending in mind.

Now, when I write about my planning this way, I do make myself sound pretty damn smart. But here's the interesting truth – all I planned was the ending. Because I knew I had that twist in mind, all the other details automatically fit in place, as I was writing. Worse than this, I had to stop part way through to try not to have an argument with my 21-year-old daughter (I failed); and finally, I didn't start writing it till 11pm on a school night. This isn't false modesty – I think the story is pretty good. However, what it does mean is that I know some basic rules which have helped me tremendously when I write. Here they are:

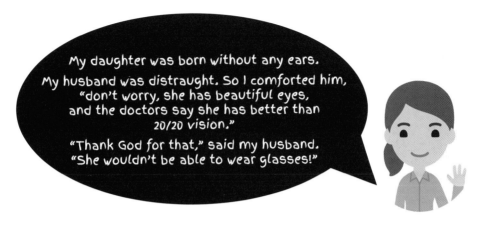

My daughter was born without any ears.

My husband was distraught. So I comforted him, "don't worry, she has beautiful eyes, and the doctors say she has better than 20/20 vision."

"Thank God for that," said my husband. "She wouldn't be able to wear glasses!"

These are my Diamond 9:

1. Start with the ending in mind
2. Show, don't tell
3. Kill your babies
4. Always include the character's or narrator's thoughts
5. Don't have more than three characters, preferably two
6. Keep the action in one place
7. Keep the action in one time
8. Plant clues that will make sense when the ending is revealed
9. Have some conflict between the two characters

What your teacher might say

There is a real problem with my advice. It may differ from your teacher's advice. This is not because either of us is a better teacher. It is because I have actually sat the exam, and your teacher probably hasn't.

For example, when your teachers looks at the requirement to have an interesting structure, they will almost definitely decide that two ways of doing this are through:
- flashback
- dual narrative

They are right, these are good ways but, are they achievable in 45 minutes under exam conditions? I don't think so. Will your teacher show you some 100% answers that can be written in that time using flashback or dual narrative? Probably not. If they can, then you can learn how to do it, and give it a go in the exam.

But I don't think these techniques will be as useful as the ones I have shown you.

The examiners also have not taken the exam

Worse than this, AQA won't show you either. If you buy their book, *Book 2 AQA GCSE English Language Assessment Preparation for Paper 1 and Paper 2*, published by Oxford University Press and written by Jane Banson and Peter Ellison, you will find that it has no stories in it, none at all. This is because even the examiners have not thought through what an actual story, written in 45 minutes might look like. They have just assumed that everybody knows, even though they can't find an example of one themselves!

I warned you that examiners are stupid.

So, if your teacher has different advice to mine, it may be better than mine, but only if they can show you a finished story where the student is likely to get a level 9.

If you do get some advice that is better than mine, please contact me on my YouTube channel, so that I can improve this guide.

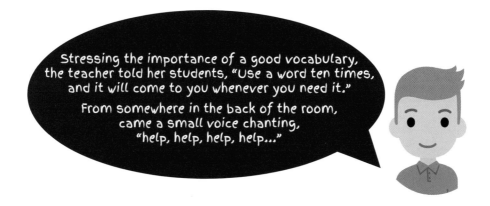

Chapter 15: Paper 2

How to get 100%

Let's get this straight – you really need to know how to recognize and use all of these rhetorical devices. These are not just for your English exam, but for life. Words persuade people. How often do you have to persuade people to help you get something you couldn't otherwise have? Weekly, daily? Got a parent? 10 or so teachers? Then you know what I mean. Now imagine it's a boss, and you can see this is a skill for life, or imagine you are a boss, and people are looking to you for leadership. Rhetorical devices will be the making of you.

Ok, so how do we remember them? I use this mnemonic:

MAD FATHERS CROCH (Rhetorical Devices, Persuasive Techniques)

Metaphor
Alliteration
Direct address
Facts
Anecdote
Triplets (Rule of Three)
Hyperbole
Emotive language
Rhetorical question
Statistics
Contrasting pairs
Repetition
Opinion
Creating an enemy
Humour

MAD FATHERS CROCH is a mnemonic. Other than that, it is not a thing. You must not write, "the author uses MAD FATHERS CROCH techniques", as there is no such thing except in this book and my classroom. MAD FATHERS CROCH is a memory tool, to help you remember rhetorical techniques. Rhetorical techniques are a thing. They were invented by the Greeks, alongside democracy and organised debate and the nude olympics. Rhetoric is how you won debates. Just like politics now, you often won debates, not by having the best evidence, but by expressing yourself best.
Get someone to test you on these as testing = learning.

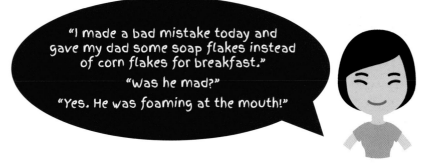

"I made a bad mistake today and gave my dad some soap flakes instead of corn flakes for breakfast."

"Was he mad?"

"Yes. He was foaming at the mouth!"

Extract from a possible exam answer

So, you would write:
 'The writer persuades through her crafting of rhetorical techniques. Her most powerful techniques are the peppering of her article with emotive language, so that her opponents are ridiculed as "misfits", "morons" and, in an inspired metaphor, "The Blob". This also allows her to portray her enemies as lesser than herself, acting on mass without thought, while she, and those who agree with her are "rational" and "logical".'

(A really good test of how far you understand this now, is to write the paragraph that exam response could have been about. You simply have to use those words in quotation marks to write a persuasive paragraph of your own).

This technique is a great way to learn, because it is challenging, and has rules. When we try to get round these strict sorts of rules, we automatically become creative. John Steinbeck used to make his children copy out passages from Dickens to learn how writers crafted their sentences. This is less creative, and I feel not as quick. His son, for example, didn't become a writer until he was 52. It worked in the long term, but did not give him a love of writing.

One of the jobs of this section of the guide is to match the hard work of writing to the reward of your producing something you feel is really good. You will enjoy being a writer. Don't just skip these activities, try them out and post them to my channel on YouTube for me to comment on.

Chapter 16: Paper 2, Question 1

To practice this question, we must use two 19th century texts. Remember, you will get a 20th or 21st century text to go with your 19th century text in the exam. However, for copyright reasons, I will avoid a modern text. This does have the added benefit for you of getting familiar with the kind of convoluted sentences older texts use, so that you will be better prepared for the exam.

Here is an example of a text from Dickens that is used in the specimen papers:

Greenwich Fair: Where Dickens let his hair down
Charles Dickens is writing in 1839 about a fair in London, which was a popular annual event he enjoyed.

The road to Greenwich during the whole of Easter Monday is in a state of perpetual bustle and noise. Cabs, hackney-coaches, 'shay' carts, coal-waggons, stages, omnibuses, donkey- chaises - all crammed with people, roll along at their utmost speed. The dust flies in clouds, ginger-beer corks go off in volleys, the balcony of every public-house is crowded with people smoking and drinking, half the private houses are turned into tea-shops, fiddles are in great request, every little fruit-shop displays its stall of gilt gingerbread and penny toys; horses won't go on, and wheels will come off. Ladies scream with fright at every fresh concussion and servants, who have got a holiday for the day, make the most of their time. Everybody is anxious to get on and to be at the fair, or in the park, as soon as possible.

The chief place of resort in the daytime, after the public-houses, is the park, in which the principal amusement is to drag young ladies up the steep hill which leads to the Observatory, and then drag them down again at the very top of their speed, greatly to the derangement of their curls and bonnet-caps, and much to the edification of lookers-on from below. 'Kiss in the Ring,' and 'Threading my Grandmother's Needle,' too, are sports which receive their full share of patronage.

Five minutes' walking brings you to the fair itself; a scene calculated to awaken very different feelings. The entrance is occupied on either side by the vendors of gingerbread and toys: the stalls are gaily lighted up, the most attractive goods profusely disposed, and un-bonneted young ladies induce you to purchase half a pound of the real spice nuts, of which the majority of the regular fair-goers carry a pound or two as a present supply, tied up in a cotton pocket- handkerchief. Occasionally you pass a deal[6] table, on which are exposed pennyworths of pickled salmon (fennel included), in little white saucers: oysters, with shells as large as cheese-plates, and several specimens of a species of snail floating in a somewhat bilious-looking green liquid.

Imagine yourself in an extremely dense crowd, which swings you to and fro, and in and out, and every way but the right one; add to this the screams of women, the shouts of boys, the clanging of gongs, the firing of pistols, the ringing of bells, the bellowings of speaking-trumpets, the squeaking of penny dittos, the noise of a dozen bands, with three drums in each, all playing different tunes at the same time, the hallooing of showmen, and an occasional roar from the wild- beast shows; and you are in the very centre and heart of the fair.

This immense booth, with the large stage in front, so brightly illuminated with lamps, and pots of burning fat, is 'Richardson's,' where you have a melodrama (with three murders and a ghost), a pantomime, a comic song, an overture, and some incidental music, all done in five-and-twenty minutes. 'Just a-going to begin! Pray come for'erd, come for'erd,' exclaims the man in the countryman's dress, for the seventieth time: and people force their way up the steps in crowds. The band suddenly strikes up and the leading tragic actress, and the gentleman who enacts the 'swell' in the pantomime, foot it to perfection. 'All in to begin,' shouts the manager, when no more people can be induced to 'come for'erd,' and away rush the leading members of the company to do the first piece.

This is about 600 words long.

Glossary
- These are closed top carriages pulled by horses
- These are open top carriages pulled by horses or donkeys
- These were large horse drawn carriages for many people. Omnibus is the origin of the word 'bus'.
- Really AQA?
- These are children's games
- A type of wood, like pine
- A plant used as a spice
- 8 short songs

What does a question look like?
Read again the first part of **source A**. Choose **four** statements below which are TRUE.

- Shade the boxes of the ones that you think are true
- Choose a maximum of four statements.

The vehicles travel quickly	( )
The ladies at the fair are on holiday for the day	( )
The favourite place for visitors to go is to the public houses	( )
The sales women do not wear bonnets	( )
The ladies do not wear bonnets	( )
Swimming snails are for sale	( )
There are at least 36 drummers	( )
Richardson's cook up bowls of fat	( )

Answers:

- The vehicles travel quickly   (True)
- The ladies at the fair are on holiday for the day   (False)
- The favourite place for visitors to go is to the public houses   (True)
- The sales women do not wear bonnets   (True)
- The ladies do not wear bonnets   (False)
- Swimming snails are for sale   (False)
- There are at least 36 drummers   (True)
- Richardson's cook up bowls of fat   (False)

Chapter 17: Paper 2, Question 2

Just tell me what to do

Let's make a checklist of what you have to do to make sure that you are comparing and inferring.

- Highlight the key words in the question, so that you are comparing the right things.
- Start your answer with this sentence to show that you are inferring; "There are similar things about (insert the key words in the question) in the two extracts **but** they have a different emphasis."
- Quote something from the oldest extract. Use "so" or "which suggests" or "which implies" to show that you are inferring something from this quotation.
- Introduce the difference with a connective: while, whereas, in contrast, on the other hand.
- Write about how this is different in the next extract, with a quotation if you can, or a direct reference if you can't.
- Quote something from the oldest extract. Use "so" or "which suggests" or "which implies" to show that you are inferring something from this quotation.
- Try to rank your differences, stating it is the main, or most dramatic, or most significant, or the worst difference. State this in your sentence.
- Make as many points as you can this way, finding differences for 12 minutes.
- Don't waste time writing a conclusion.

What does the question look like?

These quotations come from the AQA's specimen paper 2. The question is about two passages, one about the fair in Greenwhich, London, written by Charles Dickens well over 100 years ago, which you read above, and the other about the music festival at Glastonbury is an article from a broadsheet newspaper.

Question 2 will always look like this:

You need to refer to **source A** and **source B** for this question:
Use details from both sources to write a summary of the differences.

In the sample question above, the specific instruction is to look at what there is to see and do at both attractions.

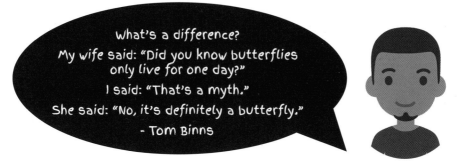

What's a difference?
My wife said: "Did you know butterflies only live for one day?"
I said: "That's a myth."
She said: "No, it's definitely a butterfly."
- Tom Binns

What the examiners really want?

This is a question in which the examiners mess up or cheat, and consequently it is very easy to lose marks. Because you could very easily write about the differences between the two passages. This would not answer the question!

For example, to make it crystal clear, the question should read "Use details from **both** sources to write a summary of these differences". Then you would know that "these" referred to the differences in what there is to "see and do".

Alternatively, they could simply ask you the question so that there is no room for doubt: "Write about the differences in what there is to see and do at Glastonbury compared to Greenwich fair."

So the first way to trip you up is the way the question ends. It is very easy for you to read the last sentence and simply write about all the differences between Glastonbury and Greenwich, not just in what there is to "see and do". My advice to students for the last 24 years is that the exam is not trying to catch you out.

With AQA, I am afraid, this is no longer true. I don't mean that the examiners are deliberately trying to catch you out. But what they, and the writers of textbooks and other revision guides don't do is try to answer the questions themselves. If they did, they would realise the questions do catch you out. So, to get the marks here you have to go back earlier in the question, and highlight the words "things to see and do".

Ok, you should highlight the key words in the question. I've told you that before. But you could still fail to get top marks, **even if you do everything that the question asks**.

What does the mark scheme say?

This is totally unfair, of course. The problem comes because the examiners want to test your ability to be "perceptive" and to "make inferences". But the question does not ask you to be perceptive or to infer. It simply asks you to state what there is to see and do at both attractions, and say how these are different.

This is what I mean by the examiners cheating you out of marks.

So, to get all the marks, we must look at the mark scheme. What you need to get 100% is an answer that looks at both texts and has:

- Perceptive interpretation
- Perceptive inferences
- Judicious references
- Perceptive differences

This means that an answer that gets all the facts right, and does exactly what the question is asking will only meet bullet points 3 and 4.

To get bullet points 1 and 2, you will have to add in interpretations that are not relevant to the question, but are relevant to the mark scheme.

These doors are alarmed.
(The windows are really startled, and the floors are very surprised).

Model answer

In the AQA mark scheme, the examiner keeps using "so" after a difference, and then adding an inference. Force yourself to use "so" as I will show you later.

However, the word "so" in your answer tells the examiner you are making an "inference". In other words, once you have quoted some evidence of what you will "see" – here different drummers – you straight away make a short, one sentence "inference" (even though this is not relevant to the question!)

How to show that you are inferring

In Band 3 you also need to infer. The exemplar for Band 3 is quite useful – the model answer points out the "main attraction" of each. This does prove that you are inferring, as the authors do not directly state which attractions are best. So, a top tip for adding inference is to rank the things you are looking at, (the key words in the question).

So, if you are asked to look at the differences in childhood, you could talk about the main differences.

- If the writers are critical, you could talk about the worst differences.
- If the writers show great differences because of the fact that the texts are say 150 years apart, you could write about the most dramatic differences.
- If the one text is really close to our own experience as a child now, we could write about the most significant difference.

Therefore, finding some way to rank the differences will show the examiner that you are inferring.

At level 2 you need to show only "some interpretation". At his level, the examiner's model shows that using the word "suggests" is enough to tell them that you are inferring.

At level 1 you still need to make sure that you are comparing.

How to start your answer to question 2

Using the examiner's comments we can also work out how to start this question.
Whatever question you get, you are guaranteed to be able to use this opening line:

"There are similar things about (insert the key words in the question) in the two extracts but they have a different emphasis."

In writing about "emphasis" you will **always** show that you are being perceptive and using inference.

Prepare for questions 2, 3 and 4 using two 19th century texts
To prepare for our exam question, read the following two texts. (Remember, you will get only one 19th century text, and a more modern one. Modern ones are subject to copyright, but also much easier, so to practise, we are going to work with the difficult texts).

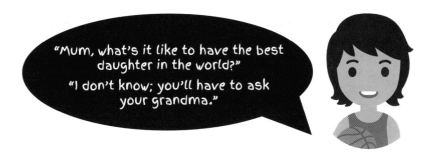

"Mum, what's it like to have the best daughter in the world?"

"I don't know; you'll have to ask your grandma."

Text A

A daughter reminiscences about Elizabeth Stuart Phelps from *Chapters from a Life* by Elizabeth Stuart Phelps [Ward]

Boston: Houghton, Mifflin and Company
The Riverside Press, Cambridge
1897 [c1896]

My mother, whose name I am proud to wear, was the eldest daughter of Professor Stuart, and inherited his intellectuality. At the time of her death she was in the first blossom of her very positive and widely-promising success as a writer of the simple home stories which took such a hold upon the popular heart. Her "Sunnyside" had already reached a circulation of one hundred thousand copies, and she was following it fast - too fast - by other books for which the critics and the publishers clamored. Her last book and her last baby came together, and killed her. She lived one of those rich and piteous lives such as only gifted women know; torn by the civil war of the dual nature which can be given to women only. It was as natural for her daughter to write as to breathe; but it was impossible for her daughter to forget that a woman of intellectual power could be the most successful of mothers.

The author of "Sunnyside", "The Angel on the Right Shoulder", and " Peep at Number Five", lived before women had careers and public sympathy in them. Her nature was drawn against the grain of her times and of her circumstances; and where our feet find easy walking, hers were hedged. A child's memories go for something by way of tribute to the achievement of one of those rare women of the elder time whose gifts forced her out, but whose heart held her in.

I can remember no time when I did not understand that my mother must write books because people would have and read them; but I cannot remember one hour in which her children needed her and did not find her.

My first distinct vision of this kind of a mother gives her by the nursery lamp, reading to us her own stories, written for ourselves, never meant to go beyond that little public of two, and illustrated in coloured crayons by her own pencil. For her gift in this direction was of an original quality, and had she not been a writer she must have achieved something as an artist.

I hardly know which of those charming ways in which I learned to spell the word motherhood impressed me most. All seemed to go on together side by side and step by step. Now she sits correcting proof-sheets, and now she is painting apostles for the baby's first Bible lesson. Now she is writing her new book, and now she is dyeing things canary-yellow in the white-oak dye-for the professor's salary is small, and a crushing economy was in those days one of the conditions of faculty life on Andover Hill. Now-for her practical ingenuity was unlimited - she is whittling ' little wooden feet to stretch the children's stockings on, to save them from shrinking; and now she is reading to us from the old, red copy of Hazlitt's "British Poets," by the register, upon a winter night. Now she is a popular writer, incredulous of her first success, with her future flashing before her; and now she is a tired, tender mother, crooning to a sick child, while the MS. lies unprinted on the table, and the publishers are wishing their professor's wife were a free woman, childless and solitary, able to send copy as fast as it is wanted. The struggle killed her, but she fought till she fell.

When I was learning why the sun rose and the moon set, how the flowers grew and the rain fell, that God and heaven and art and letters existed, that it was intelligent to say one's prayers, and that well-bred children never told a lie, I learned that a mother can be strong and still be sweet, and sweet although she is strong; and that she whom the world and her children both have need of, is of more value to each, for this very reason.

[663 words]

The 20th century text will be closer to 500 words. I shall exceed this only slightly; the greater word count will better prepare you for the exam, because you will become more expert.

"Mum, stop trying to make jokes, you know you're not funny!"

"I made you, didn't I?"

Text B
Faces We Seldom See: The Author of the Elsie Books by Florence Wilson

The author of the famous "Elsie" books has succeeded in keeping her personality hidden so completely from a curious public that it is almost as an entire stranger to her readers that THE LADIES HOME JOURNAL is able to present Miss Martha Finley.

She was born at Chillicothe, Ohio, in 1828, and for her first score or so of years, lived in different towns of Ohio and Indiana with her parents, Dr. James Brown Finley and Maria Theresa Brown. She was educated, for the most part, at home and in private schools in these different cities.

Soon after the death of her parents, about 1853, Miss Finley removed to New York, and a little later to Philadelphia, which she in turn left for Phoenixville, in the same State, and where she taught school for a number of years. During the war, and until 1874, her time was spent in either the one or the other of those places, and in the early part of 1874 – her school having been destroyed by the war – she removed to Bedford, Pennsylvania, where she made her home with an aunt and a sister. While in Philadelphia in 1876, at the Centennial Exposition, she visited relatives at Elkton, Maryland, and being in very poor health, and the surgeon whom she had selected as her physician residing there, she decided to make her home in that delightful town.

When about twenty-six years of age Miss Finley began her career as a writer, by contributing short stories to the children's departments of various Sunday school papers. Writing at first anonymously, the success of her stories induced her publishers to ask her to sign them; and as her family objected to the publishing of her own name, "Martha Farquharson" was chosen as her nom de plume. Farquharson is the clan name, the Gaelic of Finley, the family being of Scotch Irish ancestry.

Miss Finley's first successful Sunday school book was called "Jennie White." "Elsie Dinsmore," the idea of which, Miss Finley says, was given her as answer to a prayer for something which would yield her an income, was begun during the war, and with no intention of ever being continued in sequels, but the requests for the continuation have been so numerous and the demands of both public and publisher so imperative that it has never seemed possible to bring the series to a conclusion. In addition to Miss Finley's stories for children she has published several novels.

Miss Finley has been an invalid for a number of years and has done much of her writing while prostrated by illness. Despite this she keeps a bright and cheerful disposition, and is loved by all who know her.

In appearance Miss Finley is very pleasant. She is of average height with a figure inclined to plumpness. Her hair is snow white and forms a lovely setting to the delicate features and beautiful eyes beneath it. She dresses in the simplest taste, her favorite colours for her own wear being navy blue and gray.

Although the dogs of criticism have been let loose upon "Martha Farquharson" and her series of "Elsie," there has been almost no character in American juvenile fiction which has attained more widespread interest and affection. And for the author of this children's heroine there can be nothing but the kindliest feeling. In her simple womanliness and Christianity, she is a type of the best in American spinsterhood.

Ladies' Home Journal April 1893. [587 words]

Model Answer

Question 2
You need to refer to source A and source B for this question:
The behaviour and experiences of these writers was different. Use the details form both sources to write a summary of the differences.
[8 marks]

Try this question yourself first. This way, my answer will mean so much more.

I've never understood models, they're so clothes minded.

Read the model answer and try to spot the words and phrases that tell the examiner I am inferring and interpreting.

Phelps and Finley are both female writers with similar experiences of writing, but they have completely different attitudes to their work. Phelps combines writing with motherhood, as her daughter remembers "I cannot remember one hour in which her children needed her and did not find her". So perhaps this explains her desire to write children's stories "written for ourselves" (her children) and not for public consumption.

In contrast, Finley chooses to remain a "spinster" and also published books "for children", rather than keeping it for her own children. Although she has no children of her own, so she could have written them for those she taught or for those in "Sunday school".

Both women suffered from ill health. Finley seems, to a modern reader, to have little wrong with her, as she survives many years in apparent ill health: "has been an invalid for a number of years and has done much of her writing while prostrated by illness." It is unlikely that a writer could continue with serious illness, as Phelps' history indicates. Phelps died, according to her daughter, apparently from overwork, "The struggle killed her, but she fought till she fell". This is in complete contrast to Finley, who despite her claimed illness wrote many books and looked a picture of good health, with "a figure inclined to plumpness. Her hair is snow white."

This hair suggests she has lived well into old age. In contrast, Phelps has died young, "At the time of her death she was in the first blossom of her very positive and widely-promising success as a writer". Her "intellect" also suggests she would have written many more critically acclaimed books like her first few, "for which the critics and the publishers clamoured", presumably because they were so good. Most significantly, this is in contrast to Finley, who was equally popular, with "demands of both public and publisher" to write more, but without being seen as quality writing, so that "the dogs of criticism have been let loose upon "Martha Farquharson"." Perhaps this also explains why Finley published these books under a pseudonym, as though she is slightly ashamed of them. In direct contrast, Phelps is proud of her achievement, as we can infer from her daughter's pride at sharing her mother's name: "whose name I am proud to wear".

Re-read it. See if you can work out where it infers.
Below is the model answer again. The highlighting shows you where it infers.

Phelps and Finley are both female writers with similar experiences of writing, but they have completely different attitudes to their work. Phelps combines writing with motherhood, as her daughter remembers "I cannot remember one hour in which her children needed her and did not find her". So perhaps this explains her desire to write children's stories "written for ourselves" (her children) and not for public consumption.

In contrast, Finley chooses to remain a "spinster" and also published books "for children", rather than keeping it for her own children. Although she has no children of her own, so she could have written them for those she taught or for those in "Sunday school".

Both women suffered from ill health. Finley seems, to a modern reader, to have little wrong with her, as she survives many years in apparent ill health: "has been an invalid for a number of years and has done much of her writing while prostrated by illness." It is unlikely that a writer could continue with serious illness, as Phelps' history indicates. Phelps died, according to her daughter, apparently from overwork, "The struggle killed her, but she fought till she fell". This is in complete contrast to Finley, who despite her claimed illness wrote many books and looked a picture of good health, with "a figure inclined to plumpness. Her hair is snow white."

This hair suggests she has lived well into old age. In contrast, Phelps has died young, "At the time of her death she was in the first blossom of her very positive and widely-promising success as a writer". Her "intellect" also suggests she would have written many more critically-acclaimed books like her first few, "for which the critics and the publishers clamoured", presumably because they were so good.

Most significantly, this is in contrast to Finley, who was equally popular, with "demands of both public and publisher" to write more, but without being seen as quality writing, so that "the dogs of criticism have been let loose upon "Martha Farquharson"." Perhaps this also explains why Finley published these books under a pseudonym, as though she is slightly ashamed of them. In direct contrast, Phelps is proud of her achievement, as we can infer from her daughter's pride at sharing her mother's name: "whose name I am proud to wear". [379 words]

As you can see from the words in bold, each paragraph contains perceptive inference. As I move through my answer, you can see I become more confident, including more than one inference. This happens simply because I am practising the skills. This is exactly why you should practise these sorts of questions yourself – you will inevitably get better at them. Being good at English isn't about having some high degree of intelligence that other students don't have – it is simply practising the skills you need as a reader and writer.

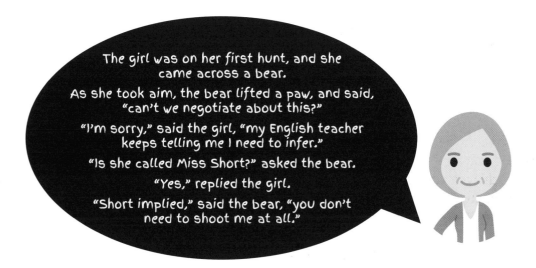

The girl was on her first hunt, and she came across a bear.

As she took aim, the bear lifted a paw, and said, "can't we negotiate about this?"

"I'm sorry," said the girl, "my English teacher keeps telling me I need to infer."

"Is she called Miss Short?" asked the bear.

"Yes," replied the girl.

"Short implied," said the bear, "you don't need to shoot me at all."

How much of my answer would you need to get 8 marks?

Phelps and Finley are both female writers with similar experiences of writing, but they have completely different attitudes to their work. Phelps combines writing with motherhood, as her daughter remembers "I cannot remember one hour in which her children needed her and did not find her". So perhaps this explains her desire to write children's stories "written for ourselves" (her children) and not for public consumption.

In contrast, Finley chooses to remain a "spinster" and also published books "for children", rather than keeping it for her own children. Although she has no children of her own, she could have written them for those she taught or for those in "Sunday school".

Both women suffered from ill health. Finley seems, to a modern reader, to have little wrong with her, as she survives many years in apparent ill health: "has been an invalid for a number of years and has done much of her writing while prostrated by illness." It is unlikely that a writer could continue with serious illness, as Phelps' history indicates. Phelps died, according to her daughter, apparently from overwork, "The struggle killed her, but she fought till she fell". This is in complete contrast to Finley, who despite her claimed illness wrote many books and looked a picture of good health, with "a figure inclined to plumpness. Her hair is snow white." [219 words]

However, your job is to write for 12 minutes – that will determine how much you can write. Practise it!

Skills

- Balanced number of quotations from each text
- 8 quotations
- 6 inferences (although 4 might be enough)

Chapter 18: Paper 2, Question 3

You now need to refer only to source B, Verne's description of The Nautilus, (line 23 to the end). How does Verne use language to make you feel the strangeness of the of the submarine?

[12 marks]

Having highlighted the key words, you will make sure that you only look at the relevant part of the text.

In the specimen paper, the question asks you to look at the feeling of being part of the fair.

(Here are just the relevant lines):

What's the difference between a submarine and an Admiral?
A sub marine isn't very good at his job.

Greenwich Fair:

Five minutes' walking brings you to the fair itself; a scene calculated to awaken very different feelings. The entrance is occupied on either side by the vendors of gingerbread and toys: the stalls are gaily lighted up, the most attractive goods profusely disposed, and un-bonneted young ladies induce you to purchase half a pound of the real spice nuts, of which the majority of the regular fair-goers carry a pound or two as a present supply, tied up in a cotton pocket- handkerchief. Occasionally you pass a deal table, on which are exposed pennyworths of pickled salmon (fennel included), in little white saucers: oysters, with shells as large as cheese-plates, and several specimens of a species of snail floating in a somewhat bilious-looking green liquid.

Imagine yourself in an extremely dense crowd, which swings you to and fro, and in and out, and every way but the right one; add to this the screams of women, the shouts of boys, the clanging of gongs, the firing of pistols, the ringing of bells, the bellowings of speaking-trumpets, the squeaking of penny dittos, the noise of a dozen bands, with three drums in each, all playing different tunes at the same time, the hallooing of showmen, and an occasional roar from the wild- beast shows; and you are in the very centre and heart of the fair.

This immense booth, with the large stage in front, so brightly illuminated with lamps, and pots of burning fat, is 'Richardson's,' where you have a melodrama (with three murders and a ghost), a pantomime, a comic song, an overture, and some incidental music, all done in five-and-twenty minutes. 'Just a-going to begin! Pray come for'erd, come for'erd,' exclaims the man in the countryman's dress, for the seventieth time: and people force their way up the steps in crowds. The band suddenly strikes up and the leading tragic actress, and the gentleman who enacts the 'swell' in the pantomime, foot it to perfection. 'All in to begin,' shouts the manager, when no more people can be induced to 'come for'erd,' and away rush the leading members of the company to do the first piece.

Just tell me what to do

- Write an opening sentence that uses the key words from the question
- Find quotations with more than one technique in them
- Use the right subject terminology when you write about them
- Remember that the descriptive techniques are always about imagery: simile, metaphor, personification, alliteration, assonance, sibilance, onomatopoeia,
- Remember that structural techniques of language are: juxtaposition, contrast, repetition, listing, complex sentences, allusion, foreshadowing.
- It is very likely that any text you meet will have all of these in 5 and 6.
- Explain what the intended effect on the reader is, for each one
- Make sure you have at least one quotation from beginning, middle and end, to show the examiner you have mastered the whole text

Model answer

Ok, now I am going to show you how to think in the exam. I will assume that every sentence has been crafted by Dickens (which it has been – that's what writers do!) My thoughts will therefore appear as bullet points after each line.

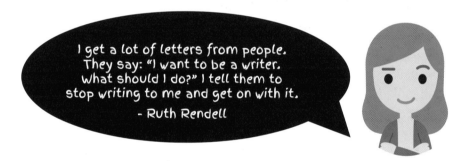

I get a lot of letters from people.
They say: "I want to be a writer.
What should I do?" I tell them to
stop writing to me and get on with it.
- Ruth Rendell

AO2:
Explain, comment on and analyse how writers use language and structure to achieve effects and influence readers, using relevant subject terminology to support their views

"Five minutes' walking brings you to the fair itself; a scene calculated to awaken very different feelings"

- Direct address places us directly at the scene
- Dickens foreshadows the text by signposting us towards different feelings to bring it to life
- He writes in the present tense to make the experience more immediate and real

"The entrance is occupied on either side by the vendors of gingerbread and toys: the stalls are gaily lighted up"

- Adjective 'gaily' to describe the lighting actually describes the mood and atmosphere
- The most attractive goods profusely disposed, and un-bonneted young ladies induce you to purchase half a
- Long clauses keep us at the scene, as though giving us time to look at the listed sights
- Perhaps male readers of the time are enticed by the provocative detail that the ladies are both "young" and "unbonneted", the adjectives suggesting they are therefore attractive.

- The assonance of "o" emphasises how "profuse" the pleasures are, and in forming the letter "o" the mouth is forced into an expression of wonder (19th century readers would be used to reading to their families out loud).
- The juxtaposition of the "young ladies" with "the most attractive goods" encourages the male reader to see the women as commodities to be enjoyed. It is a sexist allusion to women as objects.

"pound of the real spice nuts, of which the majority of the regular fair-goers carry a pound or two as a present"

- Juxtaposition of "spiced nuts" invokes the senses of smell and taste, but also asks us to consider the ladies as "spice", again reinforcing the subtle sexism.
- Supply, tied up in a cotton pocket handkerchief. Occasionally you pass a deal table, on which are exposed
- The detail of the adjective "cotton" suggest a sensory experience, where we feel ourselves carrying the nuts
- Direct address places us in the scene, but also draws us onwards as we "pass"
- The verb "exposed" comes from the same semantic field of seduction as the "young" and "unbonneted" ladies.

"pennyworths of pickled salmon (fennel included), in little white saucers: oysters, with shells as large as"

- The alliteration of "pennyworth of pickled" is reminiscent of childlike tongue twisters to emphasise the childlike pleasures of the fair
- The sibilance of "saucers", "oysters" and "shells as large as" emphasise the succulent tastes a visitor will enjoy

"Cheese-plates, and several specimens of a species of snail floating in a somewhat bilious-looking green liquid"

- The sibilance now is used for comic effect to emphasise how disgusting the "species of snail" will taste and look, appealing to the senses. This layer of disgust is not shocking, but just enough to suggest a realistic, rather than idealised portrait of the fair.
- The simile suggests that the oysters will be both tangy and filling, like a cheese course

"Imagine yourself in an extremely dense crowd, which swings you to and fro, and in and out, and every way"

- The imperative verb is a call to action, to place ourselves in the fair's heart
- The threat of overcrowding is minimised through the childlike description of the crush with the semantic field of play, so the crowd "swings you to and fro".

"but the right one; add to this the screams of women, the shouts of boys, the clanging of gongs, the firing of"

- The triplet of noise recreates the sounds of the fair in a vivid way. This time the sibilance of "screams", "shouts of boys" and "gongs" is both onomatopoeic and threatening.
- However, again, the implied audience is adult male, so they deliberately have nothing to fear from these sounds, unlike "boys" and "women".

"pistols, the ringing of bells, the bellowings of speaking-trumpets, the squeaking of penny dittos"

- Another triplet of sounds is listed, to build towards a crescendo of noise, immersing us in the scene
- The alliteration of "bells, the bellowings" creates a deeper sound, foreshadowing the sounds of the drums in the next line, and working as onomatopoeia.

"The noise of a dozen bands, with three drums in each, all playing different tunes at the same time, the"

- The alliteration of 'd' emphasises the drum beat and build toward a climax, especially if read out loud

"hallooing of showmen, and an occasional roar from the wild-beast shows, and you are in the very centre and heart of the fair."

- The long complex sentences build up a picture in layers of visual description and sound
- The position of "very" and "heart" at the end of the sentence emphasise how successfully Dickens believes he has recreated the experience of the fair for his readers to enjoy. He boastfully points out his success. (Sometimes it just gets in the way to say, "the adjective 'very' and the noun 'heart'")
- The personification of "heart of the fair" introduces us to it as a person we would like to meet, with a large and therefore good "heart".

"This immense booth, with the large stage in front, so brightly illuminated with lamps, and pots of burning"

- The description is now calmer, deliberately concentrating on sights, in contrast to the preceeding noise, which are both bright and illuminating

"fat, is 'Richardson's,' where you have a melodrama (with three murders and a ghost), a pantomime, a comic"

- The listed attractions emphasise choice
- They also appeal to the mind, suggesting what the visitor will be able to think about
- The alliteration of "m" is a gentle sound, suggesting that the "murders" and "melodrama" will both be enjoyable, and not alarming
-

"song, an overture, and some incidental music, all done in five-and-twenty minutes."

- The juxtaposition of this very short time with the huge list which led to it is deliberately comic, suggesting how enjoyable the event will be.
- This contrast also suggests that, even if the shows on offer fail to fully amuse, they will not detain the visitor for long.

Pick some from beginning, middle and end

You can see that the possibilities are everywhere. No one expects you to spot all of these, and you don't have to. You will want to show the examiner that you have an overview of the whole section they have sent you to – pick some from the beginning, middle and end.

Q: What is the longest word in the English language?

A: Smiles. (There is a mile between the first letter and the last letter.)

What does the examiner really want?

The examiner's comments on the ending:
One of the features of the AQA exemplars is the obsession with naming parts of speech. Knowing the name here adds nothing to your analysis of the effect on the reader but, an examiner under pressure will be looking for you to use these key trigger words where you quote. **Noun, adjective, verb, adverb** are terms that you must learn. It's easy marks, so learn them!

What does the mark scheme say?

- Shows detailed and perceptive understanding of language
- Analyses the effects of the writer's choices of language
- Selects a judicious range of textual detail
- Makes sophisticated and accurate use of subject terminology

What do I have to do to get 100%?
In blue, you can see all the subject terminology – nearly every quotation is accompanied with the correct terminology, to show the examiner my answer will deserve 100%.

- Shows detailed and perceptive understanding of language

Model answer (using only references with more than one techniques is really efficient)
Look back at my quotations, and find the ones where I have mentioned more than one technique. Here they are in one whole answer:

Dickens foreshadows the experience of the fair by signposting us towards "very different feelings" which will "awaken" them in the reader. Long clauses describing "stalls...goods...ladies" keep us at the scene, as though giving us time to look at the listed sights.

Perhaps Dicken's contemporary male readers are deliberately enticed by the provocative detail that the ladies are both "young" and "unbonneted", the adjectives suggesting they therefore attractive. The juxtaposition of the "young ladies" with "the most attractive goods" encourages the male reader to see the women as commodities to be enjoyed. It is a sexist allusion to women as objects. Similarly, the juxtaposition of "spiced nuts" invokes the senses of smell and taste, but also asks us to consider the ladies as "spice", again reinforcing the subtle sexism. This sexual language is also used to describe the scene, so that items on a "deal table" are described with the verb "exposed", which comes from the same semantic field of seduction as the "young" and "unbonneted" ladies.

The sibilance of "saucers", "oysters" and "shells as large as" emphasise the succulent tastes a visitor will enjoy. The sibilance now is used for comic effect to emphasise how disgusting the "species of snail" will taste and look, appealing to the senses. This layer of disgust is not shocking, but just enough to suggest a realistic, rather than idealised portrait of the fair. The simile suggests that the oysters will be both tangy and filling, like a cheese course. Sibilance is used again with a triplet of noise to recreate the sounds of the fair in a vivid way. This time the sibilance of "screams", "shouts of boys" and "gongs" is both onomatopoeic and threatening.

Another triplet of sounds is listed, "the ringing of bells, the bellowings of speaking-trumpets, the squeaking of penny dittos" to build towards a crescendo of noise, immersing us in the scene. The alliteration of "bells, the bellowings" creates a deeper sound, foreshadowing the sounds of the drums in the next line, and working as onomatopoeia. The alliteration of d's, in "the noise of a dozen bands, with three drums" emphasises the drum beat and builds toward a climax, especially if read out loud.

The listed attractions at "'Richardson's,' where you have a melodrama (with three murders and a ghost), a pantomime, a comic song" emphasise choice. They also appeal to the mind, suggesting what the visitor will be able to think about, rather than just feel. This alliteration of "m" is a gentle sound, suggesting that the "murders" and "melodrama" will both be enjoyable, and not alarming. Finally, these entertainments will "all done in five-and-twenty minutes." The juxtaposition of this very short time with the huge list which led to it is deliberately comic, suggesting how enjoyable the event will be. This contrast also suggests that, even if the shows on offer fail to fully amuse, they will not detain the visitor for long. [485 words]

(You would not need all of these in the exam – I'm just trying to show you that the writer will nearly always use more than one technique in each sentence. You would expect to write about 250 words in 18 minutes.)

Model answer
Dickens foreshadows the experience of the fair by signposting us towards "very different feelings" which will "awaken" them in the reader. Long clauses describing "stalls...goods...ladies" keep us at the scene, as though giving us time to look at the listed sights.

Perhaps Dicken's contemporary male readers are deliberately enticed by the provocative detail that the ladies are both "young" and "unbonneted". The juxtaposition of the "young ladies" with "the most attractive goods" encourages the male reader to see the women as commodities to be enjoyed. It is a sexist allusion to women as objects.

This sexual language describes the scene, so items on a "deal table" are described with the verb "exposed", which comes from the same semantic field of seduction as the "young" and "unbonneted" ladies.

The sibilance of "saucers", "oysters" and "shells as large as" emphasise the succulent tastes a visitor will enjoy. The simile suggests they will be both tangy and filling. Sibilance is used again with "screams", "shouts of boys" and "gongs", which is both onomatopoeic and threatening.

The listed attractions at "'Richardson's,' where you have a melodrama (with three murders and a ghost), a pantomime, a comic song" emphasise choice. This alliteration of "m" is a gentle sound, suggesting that the "murders" and "melodrama" will both be enjoyable, and not alarming. Finally, these entertainments will "all done in five-and-twenty minutes." The juxtaposition of this very short time with the huge list that led to it is deliberately comic, suggesting how enjoyable the event will be.

(As you can see, I try to make the same number of points, so I have a range. They are just not as detailed. I make sure they come from all parts of the text I have been directed to look at).

- Analyses the effects of the writer's choices of language

Once you get skilled at spotting techniques, you can see that many of the quotations have more than one. By simply writing about only those, you get better at finding the quotations that have most techniques in them.

In the exam, you would try to make sure that you had quotations from beginning, middle and end of the extract, so the examiner knows you have mastered it all.

The examiner can see that you are analysing, because you have more than one thing to say about each quotation. (It's ok, you can have some quotations where you say only one thing under exam pressure).

- Selects a judicious range of textual detail

Every time you write about more than one technique from a single quotation, your writing yells to the examiner – "I am judicious!"

- Makes sophisticated and accurate use of subject terminology

Every time you see a technique, you name it with the right terminology. Make sure you pick a range.

Chapter 19: Paper 2, Question 4

The question will always look like this:

> For this question, you need to refer to the whole of source A together with the whole of source B. Compare how the writers have conveyed their different views and experiences of ... (insert whatever the texts are about – places, childhood, characters, education, sport, Christmas, event, etc.)
>
> In your answer, you could:
> *   compare their different views and experiences
> *   compare the methods they use to convey those views and experiences
> *   support your ideas with references to both texts. [16 marks]

Notice that if you simply look at the bullet points you will end up answering the whole question. The most crucial word, which will ALWAYS be in question 4 is "**methods**" and this means the rhetorical devices we met earlier as MAD FATHERS CROCH (which you remember is not a thing!)

Just tell me what to do

*   Name each technique
*   Find a difference in each writer's purpose
*   Quote from each writer

In order to answer the question fully:

*   Decide on the writer's purpose.
*   Find quotations from beginning, middle and end, to show that you are referencing the whole of both texts.
*   Move through these in order

What does the mark scheme say?

A top answer:

*   Compares ideas
*   Compares perspectives
*   Is perceptive
*   Analyses writers' methods
*   Selects a range of judicious quotations
*   Is detailed

You will need to read Dickens' description of Greenwich fair, and my travel writing about Dubrovnik, below:

Dubrovnik: city of nightmares, or city of dreams?

There are few less likely victims of war. Dubrovnik's thick stone walls stand defiantly on cliff tops, cradled by mountains, an imposing and forbidding barrier to siege. Soldiers would fire down from a hundred feet up, from fortifications far taller than the puny castles you might be used to at home. Magnificent walls, the backdrop to a charming harbour.

Yet, as you walk the battlements, gasping at the beauty of the town enclosed within the womb shaped walls, you are struck by a subtle shift in colour. New, tiled roofs abound, like an orange carpet. In 1991 the Serbians attacked from the skies, dropping missiles to spread terror in this most beautiful of preserved cities. The miracle of design, three and four-foot-thick walls built to defeat earthquakes, astonishingly swallowed up the fires and explosions from the skies. The flames burnt out, starved of fuel, even where whole streets are only about eight feet apart.

So yes. Dubrovnik is something of a miracle, a survivor with its whole history intact.

But there is something unnatural about it, like having a baby that comes out 50 years old: smart, articulate, affluent, but very, very wrong.

Most of the streets are lanes, cramped and crowded with tables, even before the tourists arrive. And they descend in coach loads, piling through the Pile gate, swarming like locusts on a ripe field. They block every intersection as guides drone on in a dozen languages, clogging the city's arteries.

The cafes are bursting with foreign wealth, jacking up the cost of a sandwich to £10, a beer for £6. Peace and quiet? Not even money can buy you that. The narrow streets cast everything in shadow, so you bake in the heat without the benefit of sunshine.

As you stumble from alley to alley, dodging the maître Ds trying to pimp their restaurants to you, hurdling the hundreds of stray cats swarming at your feet, you look up and notice every building looks the same, exactly four stories high, in bland limestone. No one is allowed to paint a single brick, never mind a wall.

You try to find some space in a bigger building, the Rector's palace, or the Natural History Museum. First you find they are overpriced, and that's before the pound plummeted. Then you find you are not allowed to take photographs. You go in anyway, to find space to breathe, and escape the noise and crowds. The star exhibits are 120 stuffed birds. No, really. This is beyond a joke. And the Rector seems to have been especially proud of a collection of treasure chests, all open, proudly displaying their emptiness to you. Yes, like your wallet, they once held riches, which are now no more than memories.

No matter. Dubrovnik boasts 313 restaurants, and you still have a credit card. Unfortunately, you don't like fish, and everywhere serves fish. This explains the cats, and the smell. Even when you find a table, built for child-sized frames, in order to maximise places and profits, and you tuck in to your delicious meatballs in green curry sauce, does your mouth water? Yes, but meanwhile your nose twitches and runs, as the couple next to you are eating muscles and squid, reeking of garlic and the sea, while behind you four girlfriends are shrieking through cocktails and cigarettes. Yes, smoking is a national sport, and the Croatians are very good at it indeed. They are a proud nation, so they practise everywhere. Finally, you try to drown your sorrows. A glass of wine, sir? Certainly, please try one of our dozen Croatian wines. Yes, just Croatian wines sir. No matter, the menu boasts some brilliant Belgian beer. Your spirits lift: the crowds and smoked filled clouds recede. Ah, sorry, end of season sir. We have only Croatian beer, fizzy and flavourless.

So, you plod wearily home, shuffling down the wrong alley, because they all look the same. At last you find your door and climb wearily to bed. Raucous Karaoke breaks out from the bars beneath. You look for double glazing, but it is probably as forbidden as paint. You shut the shutters. Then the windows. The songs keep rising like a midnight tide.

You shut your eyes and dream of home.

Model answer

Dominic Salles uses direct address to take the reader on a journey around the city, "as you walk the battlements". While Salles tours this city, Dickens uses direct address to take the reader to the centre of Greenwich fair, "imagine yourself… in the very centre and heart of the fair."

Both writers therefore experience the city on foot. This metaphor, and the positive connotations of "heart", imply that the fair will be a joyous experience. Salles begins with similar praise, using the hyperbole of the reader "gasping at the beauty of the town." However, Salles takes the reader on a series of experiences which will make the reader wish to leave.

Thus the alliteration of "cramped and crowded" lanes emphasises how little you might enjoy walking the streets. He uses the threatening simile of tourists "swarming like locusts" to convey his horror at being trapped in the crowds.

In contrast, Dickens celebrates being in "an extremely dense crowd", using language from the semantic field of play, so that the crowd "swings you to and fro" like a game, before delivering you to the "centre".

The sounds are brought to life by Dickens through the alliteration of "bells, the bellowings" and the sibilance of "this the screams of women, the shouts of boys". While this might sound uncomfortable, the implied reader appears to be male, and the adult males do not scream here.

Salles uses sounds to convey the opposite. The alliteration of "guides drone on in a dozen languages" recreates his frustration at the constant, unintelligible chatter, and the verb "drone" further suggests his boredom. He also uses sibilance to describe the cats, the effect of which, perhaps, is to recreate the sound of their hissing: "hundreds of stray cats swarming."

Salles relies heavily on contrast, juxtaposing what he would like to experience against the reality, so "you don't like fish, and everywhere serves fish." Dickens also juxtaposes the apparent riches of the "melodrama… The pantomime, a comic song" and more, with the almost absurd ending of the paragraph, "all done in five in 20 minutes."

Salles also uses humour to illustrate that there is no relief, so that the "star exhibits" of "120 stuffed birds" is "beyond a joke". The difference is that Salles feels trapped in the city, "shuffling down the wrong alley", while Dickens feels enticed by the show, even though the compare calls "come for'erd… For the seventieth time". This hyperbole conveys his pleasure at the show.

Salles ends his ordeal with a simile to describe the incessant noise of the "Raucous Karaoke" with songs that "keep rising like a midnight tide." This simile conveys his growing sense of panic at being trapped in the city. The addition of the adjective "midnight" also has connotations of evil, so that the darkness of night is not welcoming.

In contrast, Dickens chooses to end with an image of perfection, emphasised by assonance and alliteration, all at once. The layering of these techniques also suggest the "perfection", mirroring the well-crafted show he describes, "the gentleman who enacts the 'swell' in pantomime, foot it to perfection". The alliterative T's actually sound out the dancer's feet, like tapping on the stage.

(530 words in 24 minutes)

Model answer explained

(You should have realised why learning the persuasive rhetorical techniques was so useful. MAD FATHERS CROCH is essential for answering this question, and question 5).

Dominic Salles uses direct address to take the reader on a journey around the city, "as you walk the battlements". While Salles tours this city, Dickens uses direct address to take the reader to the centre of Greenwich fair, "imagine yourself... in the very centre and heart of the fair."

- Name the technique – here "direct address".
- State how one writer uses it differently to the other.
- Quote from each writer.

Both writers therefore experience the city on foot. This metaphor, and the positive connotations of "heart", imply that the fair will be a joyous experience. Salles begins with similar praise, using the hyperbole of the reader "gasping at the beauty of the town." However, Salles takes the reader on a series of experiences which will make the reader wish to leave.

- Name the techniques – here metaphor and hyperbole.
- Although the techniques are different, they are linked together with the same purpose – to praise.
- Find a difference within this – here the writers' purposes.
- Quote from each writer.

Thus the alliteration of "cramped and crowded" lanes emphasises how little you might enjoy walking the streets. He uses the threatening simile of tourists "swarming like locusts" to convey his horror at being trapped in the crowds.

In contrast, Dickens celebrates being in "an extremely dense crowd", using language from the semantic field of play, so that the crowd "swings you to and fro" like a game, before delivering you to the "centre".

- Name the techniques – here alliteration, simile, semantic field.
- Discuss the difference – here the writer's purpose.
- Quote from each writer.

The sounds are brought to life by Dickens through the alliteration of "bells, the bellowings" and the sibilance of "this the screams of women, the shouts of boys". While this might sound uncomfortable, the implied reader appears to be male, and the adult males do not scream here.

Salles uses sounds to convey the opposite. The alliteration of "guides drone on in a dozen languages" recreates his frustration at the constant, unintelligible chatter, and the verb "drone" further suggests his boredom. He also uses sibilance to describe the cats, the effect of which, perhaps, is to recreate the sound of their hissing: "hundreds of stray cats swarming."

- Name the techniques – here alliteration, sibilance.
- Discuss the difference – here the authors' purposes.
- Quote from each writer.

You work out the rest!

The other skill of the answer is that it shows that the student has considered the whole of Text A and the whole of Text B by looking at the endings.

"I met a painter who only paints using Japanese rice wine, but it was just saké for art's sake." - Phil Mann

What is a writer's tone?

On the specimen papers, tone might be relevant to questions 2 and 3, and will always be relevant to questions 4 and 5. This is because the whole paper is about writers' viewpoints – and viewpoints are always conveyed through tone. Questions 4 and 5 carry 56 out of 80 marks, so 70%! You really need to be able to describe and create tone.

All writers have a point of view or purpose. Writers use their tone to reveal this point or view, or purpose.

For example, go back and look at Phelp's memories of her mother, and decide on both her purposes and her tone.

The tone of Phelps' piece was celebratory, positive and eulogising. She celebrates both her mother's achievements as a writer, but also her sacrifice and warmth as a mother. She sees her mother as a positive role model to all modern women, who don't suffer the same hardships. It is written after her mother's death and so is a eulogy, celebrating her life.

From these tones we can infer several purposes:
- To celebrate her mother, and her mother's writing.
- To reintroduce a reading public to her after her books have been forgotten.
- To promote herself and her own achievements following in her mother's footsteps.
- To educate modern female readers in particular about the sacrifices made by the female generation that preceded them.
- To accuse society, and perhaps by extension her father, who forced her mother to do too much, when it should have allowed her to develop entirely as a writer.

You can see from this that a top answer will consider more than one purpose, and more than one tone. You won't need all of them!

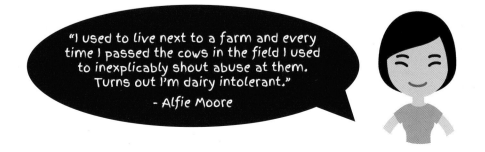

"I used to live next to a farm and every time I passed the cows in the field I used to inexplicably shout abuse at them. Turns out I'm dairy intolerant."
- Alfie Moore

Look beneath the writing: this is where the author is hiding

Sophisticated readers look at the apparent purpose of a piece of writing, but then look underneath at the writer's deeper purpose.

For example, if you look at my short story about my mother, in paper 1, the purpose is obviously to interest you in my childhood experiences. However, you might have a number of questions about tone:

- Is it a forgiving or an accusatory tone?
- Are our memories and differences reconciled at the end?
- If I end with "we" instead of "you" am I hinting that I also got things wrong?
- Do I do this to make my mother seem better than she was?
- Am I after a happy ending, or are feelings unresolved?
- How far is my audience you, the reader, and how much is it my mother?
- How far am I trying to understand my mother, compared to how far I want you to understand me?
- How far is it a lesson (I am a teacher after all) to cherish your parents while you can, no matter the mistakes they make in bringing you up?

Now you have considered this, is the tone accusatory or part eulogistic? Is it moralistic, trying to teach a lesson? Is it nostalgic, trying to recreate a past to celebrate it? Is it sad, looking back with regret, or happy, reconciling the past with the present?

By dealing with this as questions, I am trying to show you what expert readers do. These questions, and many others, continually fire in the readers' mind. This is what it means to be fully engaged with the text, so that you inhabit it. You don't just see the world described in it, but you also look around for traces of the writer.

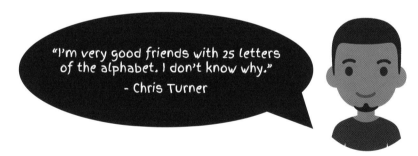

"I'm very good friends with 25 letters of the alphabet. I don't know why."
- Chris Turner

The author is dead (so we can't ask what they meant)

The most common question I get from students is: surely, the author didn't think about this when they wrote it? They can't possibly have thought about every sentence, the way we are analyzing it, can they?

Well, the answer, I am afraid, is that they probably have. They will have written numerous drafts, chopping, changing, crossing things out and revising. They will have obsessed about every sentence.

Some writers deny this level of thought, because readers ask them "what does it really mean?" This is because they want you to find your own meaning in the text. Writers are readers first, and they want you to think hard about reading.

There are all kinds of interpretations that are possible for any text. We can never enter into the author's mind and be certain what was there, even the author can't. Expert readers assume that the author is dead and so we just look at the words on the page and ask what they suggest to us. The text carries all the meaning, even if we interpret it in a way that the author never intended. Get used to it.

The other lesson I am teaching through these questions is that many of your answers will be contradictory. You are not seeking a truth about the author that everyone will agree on, even the author. Instead, you are looking for clues and patterns that make sense to you. The reason I've based these questions on my own writing is to show you that the authors often do not know the exact answer themselves. In other words, to find meaning in the text, you enter into a kind of conversation between you and the imaginary author.

Chapter 20: Paper 2, Section B

Just tell me what to do

Writing to persuade or argue or inform

5-minute plan:
- Outline the issue
- Argument
- Counter argument
- (As many arguments and counterarguments as you can fit in the time)
- Concluding argument
  a. Include in this long term consequences, seeing far (years or generations) into the future (most candidates won't do this)
  b. A call to action using imperative verbs.

Write

These are exactly the same skills you practised in the narrative and description in paper 1, question 5:
- Start each sentence in a different way
- Show off with your vocabulary
- Show off with your control of sentences
  - Really short sentences for tension
  - A curtailed sentence (without a verb) for emphasis of drama
  - Long, complex and convoluted sentence to layer description and information
- Show off with your control of paragraphing
  - A short, one sentence paragraph
  - A long one sentence paragraph
  - Mirror the sentence structure of one paragraph in another
- Show off with your control of punctuation
  - Commas, colons, semi-colons, dashes, brackets

'MAD FATHERS CROCH'
Use these rhetorical devices in every sentence. Even better, use several per sentence.

What does the examiner want?

Paper 2 rewards the same skills as question 5 on paper 1. However, in this paper, you will never be asked to describe or narrate. Instead, you will "**explain, instruct, give and respond to information, and argue**".
The examiners say "You are advised to spend about 45 minutes on this section".

- Write in full sentences
- You are reminded of the need to plan your answer
- You should leave enough time to check your work at the end

How to plan non-fiction writing

The first thing I would suggest is that good writers don't plan. Because they write about what they know, and because they know how texts are structured, there is no need to plan.

I didn't plan any of the non-fiction writing you will find in this guide. These are all exam answers, which I wrote under exam conditions. You need to practise writing under exam conditions until you don't need to plan.

Let me explain. When I wrote on Dubrovnik or "Countdown to Grammar Schools", or "What is the Purpose of Education?" I did not have to plan my facts. I already knew them. I did not need to work out which order to write my paragraphs, because I knew that my first paragraph had to outline the issue, and the final paragraphs had to put forward my most powerful and persuasive reasons.

I knew all my other paragraphs had to link logically, because the basic structure was a conversation with an imaginary listener in my head. Texts do this simply: argument, counter argument, argument, counter argument…

> Q: How many planning officers does it take to change a lightbulb?
>
> A: None, planners don't change anything.

This follows the exact same structure you are used to hearing in school, but with much better vocabulary:

Argument:	I told her that…
Counter argument:	And can you believe that she said…
Argument:	Now I know I can be wrong, but this time I was so right, so I said…
Counter argument:	And she had the cheek to say…
Argument:	So I didn't hold back, I told her…
Counter argument:	She tried to argue back with…
Argument:	So then I reminded her about…
Conclusion:	And she shut up because…

To build to this level of confidence, your plan to advise or persuade will be as above:

- Outline the issue
- Argument
- Counter argument
- (As many as you can fit in the time)
- Concluding argument

- Include in this long term consequences, seeing far into the future (most candidates won't do this)
- A call to action using imperative verbs.

What does the mark scheme say?

The mark scheme is exactly the same as for paper 1, question 5:

AO5 Content and Organisation

- Communicate clearly, effectively and imaginatively, selecting and adapting tone, style and register for different forms, purposes and audiences.
- Organise information and ideas, using structural and grammatical features to support coherence and cohesion of texts.

For 22-24 marks:

Assessment Objective 5

Content
- Register is convincing
- Everything matches your purpose
- Ambitious vocabulary with lots of linguistic devices

Organisation
- Inventive structural features
- Convincing and complex ideas
- Fluently linked paragraphs

AO6 Technical Accuracy

Candidates must use a range of vocabulary and sentence structures for clarity, purpose and effect, with accurate spelling and punctuation.

For 13 to 16 marks:
- Sentence demarcation is consistently secure and consistently accurate
- Wide range of punctuation is used with a high level of accuracy
- Uses a full range of appropriate sentence forms for effect
- Uses Standard English consistently and appropriately with secure control of complex grammatical structures
- High level of accuracy in spelling, including ambitious vocabulary
- Extensive and ambitious use of vocabulary

To get in the top band, your writing needs to be "compelling and convincing". This is marked in two areas:

Your simplified writing assessment checklist

Use an imaginative structure
Use lots of techniques, and use them originally
Show off with vocabulary
Show off with different types of sentences
Show off with a range of punctuation

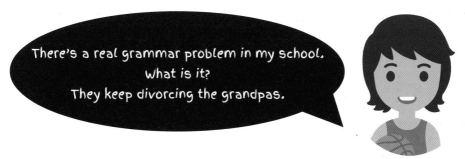

There's a real grammar problem in my school.
What is it?
They keep divorcing the grandpas.

Writing to argue and persuade

Below is an article I wrote for Schools Improvement, which was published at: http://schoolsimprovement.net/grammar-school-perspectives-dominic-salles/

It was commissioned to add to the debate about whether we should create many more grammar schools. See if you can find the techniques from MAD FATHERS CROCH.

Countdown to grammar schools

I'll have an opinion please Rachel. And a hyperbole. And another hyperbole. Yes, now an opinion.

Michael, you have a six-letter word: Brexit. Congratulations. Yes, it is now in the dictionary. And Theresa, you have a seven-letter word: grammar, where would we be without it? Congratulations, you are today's winner.

And so we sprint towards an uncertain future, stiffened by the shouts of opinion and hyperbole: parents of progress or decline? The countdown clock will tell.

But what if we count up, instead of down? What if we looked at some numerical facts about grammar schools? What if, unlike the fact-free Brexit debate, everything we needed to know were contained in one place, indeed, one spreadsheet? Welcome, ladies and gentlemen, to the Gov.uk performance tables. Make yourselves at home in a world of facts.

Opinion 1: grammar schools increase social mobility.
Fact: The number of disadvantaged students in Year 11 in selective schools in 2015 was 1389, 4% of their Year 11. Social mobility, or mobility scooter? How do these students do? With these cherry picked few, 89% make expected progress in English, and similarly in maths. Not shabby. So, for disadvantaged students, grammar schools could work, if only they could push through the weighted doors. We need to dramatically increase their number.

Opinion 2: brighter students do better at grammar school.
Fact: Grammar schools select the very best from among high attaining students, whereas around 40% are high attaining (getting level 5 at KS2) across comprehensives. In 46% of grammars, more than 95% of high attainers make expected progress. But 21% make 90% or less: a fifth of grammar schools are pretty poor, because expected progress is a B. You don't spend a fortune on house prices or tutors for B grades. Nobody hangs their dreams on a B.

Would you expect an average of an A grade? 53% of selective schools average an A minus or below. That means their 'average' child is getting 6 As and 5 Bs. More mediocrity than meritocracy. Selective schools' mean value added is 1023.2. Yet there are 206 comprehensives with better than this mean, more than the country's 162 selective schools.

Disappointingly, this represents only 7% of comprehensives. Conversely, five comprehensives have higher value added for high attainers than the best grammar school. Difficult to interpret. But think of your home town. There are 24 secondaries within 15 miles of my home (34 within 20 miles). How many of their students would gain ten A* to As? Enough to fill a grammar cohort? Definitely: an A minus average is a very poor return.

Opinion 3: they promote excellence.
Fact: These figures suggest that, at most, 50% of grammar schools do well by their students. This pretends there is no effect from tutors, parental support, the hot house effect of creaming off the very best (many successful grammar schools compete with other grammars, taking their best students). Shouldn't we close grammar schools where students average below an A-?

Opinion 4: they are better than the comprehensive alternative.
Fact: It is impossible to compare the broad level 5 student in a comprehensive to the narrower range admitted to grammars. But it is true that over 90% of comprehensives have level 5 students doing worse than they do at grammar schools. Conversely 186 comprehensives get A- to A+ as an average grade for high attainers, easily outnumbering the total of all selective schools. Interestingly, Theresa May's plans will allow these schools to become grammar schools themselves. A further 1494 comprehensive get the same average B and B+ grades that the bottom fifth of grammar schools achieve. That's 1678 grammar school equivalents for parents to choose from, already right here, no magic wand required.

So, are grammars an elitist con, pretending to meritocracy? No, that's not the problem.

The problem is that they are not elitist enough. The problem is their collective expectations are simply too low. Let's transform grammar schools, and have more of them. Let's have elitist, ambitious selection criteria for all existing, and new grammar schools. An entrance exam, or a top 15% national score in the new KS2 tests, which all must reach. Pupil premium money for the best tutoring at KS1 and 2.

Let's demand social mobility. First admission to the disadvantaged, make it 40%, still less than double the national average. Next admit those whose family income is below £40,000. And then those who own property valued below £300,000. And then any EAL student in the top 25% of all students nationally (because they catch up). And now, if there are still places to fill, let's let in the middle classes, by distance from the school. Remember, there are at least 1678 comprehensive schools where the rejected middle classes are likely to do just as well. Real choice.

So, let's make the next generation the brave heirs to Maggie and Michael and May. Count me in, Rachel.

Let's have a look at how the rhetorical techniques are used:
Test yourself on the mnemonic, MAD FATHERS CROCH first, because you've learned it, right?

Countdown to grammar schools
I'll have an opinion please Rachel. And a hyperbole. And another hyperbole. Yes, now an opinion... (repetition)

Michael, you have a six-letter word: Brexit. Congratulations. Yes, it is now in the dictionary. And Theresa, you have a seven-letter word: grammar, where would we be without it? Congratulations, you are today's winner. **(Anecdote and humour)**

And so we sprint towards an uncertain future, stiffened by the shouts of opinion and hyperbole: parents of progress or decline? The countdown clock will tell. **(Several metaphors, using emotive language, alliteration, contrasting pairs)**

But what if we count up, instead of down? What if we looked at some numerical facts about grammar schools? What if, unlike the fact-free Brexit debate, everything we needed to know were contained in one place, indeed, one spreadsheet? Welcome, ladies and gentlemen, to the Gov.uk performance tables. Make yourselves at home in a world of facts. **(Rhetorical questions, rule of three, creating an enemy, alliteration, emotive language, direct address, metaphor)**

Opinion 1: grammar schools increase social mobility.
Fact: The number of disadvantaged students in Year 11 in selective schools in 2015 was 1389, 4% of their Year 11. Social mobility, or mobility scooter? How do these students do? With these cherry-picked few, 89% make expected progress in English, and similarly in maths. Not shabby. So, for disadvantaged students, grammar schools could work, if only they could push through the weighted doors. We need to dramatically increase their number. **(fact and opinion, statistics, metaphor, contrasting pairs, emotive language, metaphor, direct address)**

By this stage, then, I have already used all the rhetorical techniques in MAD FATHERS CROCH. That's in the first 215 words. You have 45 minutes, in which you ought to be able to write double this length. If you practise using these techniques, one at a time, they will become second nature to you.

Here is an interesting fact for you. Yes, I am an English teacher, but I have only been commissioned to write articles since I published my book in August 2016. In other words, the only training I have had in using these techniques is teaching them in class. This means that over the course of Year 10 and 11 you can practise them at least as many times as I have.

The best technique I can suggest is that you try these at random. For this, you pick something you either feel passionately about or one that is just ridiculous. Both of these will allow you just to concentrate on the techniques.

In class I do this one minute at a time, one minute for each technique. For example, you are going to argue that all houses should be round instead of square. Or that we should vote for monkeys instead of politicians, or that elephants should replace the car. Then you start with any letter from MAD FATHERS CROCH. Let's say A=alliteration. Then your next sentence must be S=statistics. Your next after that will be a sentence with E=emotive language. Because this is so artificial, you quickly forget about what you are writing and focus entirely on mastering the techniques. You will get better very quickly.

Random topics to help you practice

- We should all live in round houses
- We should abandon the motor car and take to the elephant
- Global warming is brilliant; we need more of it
- We should vote for monkeys instead of politicians
- Only women should have jobs and men should stay at home with the children

In your exam preparation, you should try the first two with a plan, and the next two without planning. You should find a happy balance where you discover how far you need to plan in the exam.

Q: Why do elephants paint their privates red?
A: So they can hide in cherry trees.
Q: What's the loudest noise in the jungle?
A: An elephant at cherry picking time.

What does a question look like?

Question 5 will always introduce a statement, and always ask you to agree or disagree with it. It won't ask you to get splinters in your buttocks by sitting on the fence. Make a choice, and argue it!

Question 5:

"Homework has limited benefits. It is absolutely right that schools should make homework optional."

Write an article for an educational website in which you argue for all against this statement.

(24 marks for content and organisation, 16 marks for technical accuracy, 40 marks)

Three A* (or Level 8 and 9 techniques) for persuasive and argumentative writing
They are:

Argue the least popular view

Make 'creating an enemy' your dominant technique

Use humour to ridicule the enemy – e.g. those who oppose your view

(You will see how to do this in my model answer at the end of this section)

It is possible that the topic you will be given to write about in paper 2 will be predictable, because there are only so many things that all Year 11s can be expected to know about. However, because it will be based on ideas in the two texts studied I the exam, and because one of these will be a 19th century text, it is equally possible that the topic will be unpredictable. For example, one sample paper asks you to write about the benefits of travel during school time, which you have probably given very little thought to.

However, this does suggest that the most likely topics will always be related to teenagers lives. Let's see if we can predict some tired old questions.

Should schools:
- Get rid of uniform
- Ban electronic devices
- Have a longer school day
- Have shorter holidays
- Get rid of homework

About parenting. Should parents:
- Encourage part time work
- Monitor children's online use
- Pay their children by results in exams
- Take children out of school for holidays

Here are some more interesting questions about school. Should schools:
- Offer parenting classes
- Invite parents to learn with their children
- Allow children to teach themselves from the internet
- Be online, so hundreds of students could be taught at the same time
- Insist all students eat together
- Pay teachers based on the results of their students
- Teach everyone a language and a musical instrument
- Have lessons from eight till six, with teenagers starting the school day later, at ten

One thing is clear. The examiners are no longer going to ask you a question that relies on your having any kind of general knowledge, or being well read. This causes a problem. How will good candidates show that they are particularly good if the question is tedious and undemanding?

Well, 90% of the answer is showing off in the ways I have taught you. Some guides give you **Arrested** or **Daforest** as mnemonics. You have the much more expert **Mad Fathers Croch**.

The final 10% difference is in your approach to the question. Try to choose a response that no one else will give. So you will be in favour of homework, school uniform, banning technology in schools. You won't want to do this, so practise with these three questions and post your answers to me on YouTube.

The worst speller in my class came back from the toilet.

"How many times, Jess, your shirt's out again," I said.

Red faced, she backed out of the room, looking for toilet paper.

Let's try one with school uniform. Imagine the question:

> "Uniform has limited benefits. It is absolutely right that students should be allowed to wear their own clothes to school."

> Write an article for an educational website in which you argue for all against this statement.

> (24 marks for content and organisation, 16 marks for technical accuracy, 40 marks)

Model answer

So you want to get rid of school uniform. Perhaps Daddy and Mummy are rich, rich, rich and you want to show us all your designer gear, parading an endless range of just-off-the-shelf splendour and fashion to make your friends praise you and your rivals sick with envy.

Direct address, emotive language, anecdote, rule of three, contrasting pairs, metaphor. Creating an enemy.
Or perhaps you love lounging about at home in your sportswear, festooned with the right labels, hats and trainers still with their price tags proudly displayed, a sea of pristine white, kept shop-display neat.

Repetition, alliteration, anecdote, emotive language, metaphor. Creating an enemy.
Or perhaps you have other tribes: you are a goth, an emo, you're indie, a hipster, you're a dude, a dudette, a geek, a gangsta, or some other made up group you're so desperate to belong to in your teenage years before adult life 'ruins' it all.

Hyperbole, repetition, direct address, rule of three, emotive language, metaphor, alliteration. The opening three paragraphs create an enemy through humour.
As we can see, the main arguments against uniform are anti-education. They are all to do with display and social status. They all say, "this is not a school, this is social media made flesh and designer thread." Who would place learning first in such an environment?

Direct address, opinion, contrasting pairs, alliteration, repetition, metaphor, rhetorical question.
Moreover, let's pretend for a minute that these competing tribes wouldn't be revealed, that students would dress sensibly in less branded clothes. Let's pretend that students would find their own casual work wear and that schools would become, well, a place of work.

Emotive language, metaphor, repetition, anecdote.
How many girls would choose to display distracting amounts of cleavage and thigh as puberty takes hold? Three, four or five in a class of 14 and 15-year-old boys, whose spike in hormones has already given them the equivalent of X-ray vision. With every hormone pumped into their blood stream screaming at them to pass on their DNA as quickly as possible, what hope would boys have of a great education? Hello, has anyone noticed how boys are already being left behind by the hard working determination of girls? Worse than this, how will we educate boys not to harass girls out of school, when they are bombarded with temptation at school?

Rhetorical questions, emotive language, statistics, fact, metaphor, humour, personification, contrasting pairs.
And now consider the effect on girls. The rise in their anxiety, self-harm and eating disorders in schools has reached epidemic proportions. Let me ask you: will forcing girls to fixate and obsess on the right clothing to display help cure this epidemic, or spread it like a plague?

Emotive language, rule of three, rhetorical question, direct address, alliterations, contrasting pairs.

We all know these are rhetorical questions.

Now, without worrying about what to wear, each student is equally able to excel. The poorer student is no longer labelled, but able to learn as well as anyone else. Both genders can express themselves through learning music, drama, art and sport, skills which will enrich them for life, in contrast to fashion which will change over a weekend.

Boys and girls can truly focus on learning, rather than signaling social and sexual status. They will gain long term education instead of short term kudos from fashion.

Yes, teachers will no doubt fixate on whether a top button is done up, or a shirt is tucked in. But treasure those moments. It means the idiots in your class are not throwing your books around the room, or constantly interrupting your learning with an endless series of coughs, questions, pen and ruler trappings, prodding other pupils and swearing. Their rebellion is focused on untucking the front of their shirt, and you can get on with learning, preparing for your degree, investing in your future.

Yes, with a proper school uniform, even the students who don't want to learn will learn so much more. Meanwhile, the rest of you will be released from the dictatorships of tribes and fashion; you will all be free to thrive. Choose the freedom to succeed. [609 words]

In italics are the techniques from MAD FATHERS CROCH when each first appears. They've all been used, often several times, in the first 338 words, without my being conscious of which ones I have used. I simply try to show off in every sentence.

I deliberately chose this because I am not in favour of school uniform. Research shows uniform has no effect on students' academic progress, so I can take it or leave it, and I spend far too much of my day reminding students about it. This therefore allows me to show you how arguing a point of view you don't agree with liberates you to show off. Better than this, it forces you to show off.

"People say I've got no willpower but I've quit smoking loads of times."

Writing to inform

This is a bog standard writing to inform piece.

Mr. Salles is not writing this guide to make money. To do this he would have to dumb it down, and include lots of tips on how to achieve levels 4, 5 and 6.

This would vastly increase the number of potential readers of this guide. However, Mr. Salles believes that all students should strive to be excellent. He believes that all students are capable of getting much higher than their predicted grades. Consequently, his guide has a complete focus on how to achieve the highest grades.

Mr. Salles also believes that the best way to achieve a level 5 or 6 is not to be taught those skills alone. Instead, reading about how to get levels 7, 8 and 9, will develop your skills in lots of ways. True, most students won't leap to levels 8 and 9. However, most of them will develop some level 8 and 9 skills. This will make them, and you, better readers and writers. This will also mean that when examiners look for a "best fit" they will improve your level, at least from 4 to 5, from 5 to 6, 6 to 7 etc.

Mr. Salles explains that, though this can be hard for students to do, if they keep practising, improvement is inevitable. He urges you to keep going, and send your attempts to him at his YouTube channel, Mr. Salles Teaches English. Hundreds of students post comments each year, thanking him for his videos that have helped them achieve the highest grades, and do much better than they or their teachers expected. His channel has had well over 1 million views. This guide will take your revision to new levels. [280 words]

Features of writing to inform:
- Includes facts and statistics
- The tone will be formal
- The language will be formal

- Opinions will be hidden and pretending to be facts
- Sentences tend to start with a connective
- Extra information is often added in parenthesis, e.g. in the middle of the sentence. It is also frequently added as a subordinate clause at the beginning or end of the sentence. This is because the writer wants to show how facts or ideas are connected.
- You will see that these are organisational features which are very similar to persuasive or argumentative texts. This is because informative texts often try to persuade you with facts: buy this revision guide, work hard, do brilliantly.

Why wouldn't this piece get 100%?
- It's too short for 40 minutes of writing
- Too many paragraphs start the same way
- Too many sentences start the same way
- There are few rhetorical devices (MAD FATHERS CROCH)
- Although it shows off with commas, it doesn't show off other punctuation
- Although the beginning is a little original, the ending isn't
- Paragraphs are organized, but not crafted for impact

100% model

Every actor wants to be Tom Cruise, and every actress longs to be Jennifer Lawrence. So why settle for Danny Dyer and Letitia Dean? You wouldn't, and shouldn't. It's exactly the same thing with revision guides. Yes, they come with pretty pictures, and jokes, and everything is chunk sized so that it fits a single page. But do they push you, pull you, and propel you to get an A or an A*? You've spotted that's a rhetorical question, but do you know the other 14 rhetorical devices? Mr Salles won't just list them; by the time you finish this guide, you will know them by heart. Fact.

Mr Salles believes that all students can ace the English language exam; that every student can learn from beyond A* answers that are properly explained; that every student can remember if they are shown how. Ambition is his recurring theme. He is desperate for you to do well, and shows you exactly how to excel.

Surprising insights will allow you to view the exam in a new way, so that you move from the simple, sit-back-and-enjoy-the-show kind of guide, to a 3D extravaganza where you learn what is in the examiner's head, learn how to dazzle by showing off your own skills, and learn how to give the examiner no choice but to throw marks at your answers.

Mr Salles' YouTube channel has saved many students from bog standard teaching, or from annoying classes who refuse to let you learn at pace. This guide allows you to teach yourself, and you can dip into it at any level. Those in a hurry will sprint through the 'just tell me what I need to know' sections (surely the most useful 10 pages of any guide on the market); those who are desperate to see what the new levels 8 and 9 look like will relish the more than a dozen 100% answers and those that want to become expert writers and readers will marvel at the range of writers and texts to practise on. If you are someone who loves reading, and would love to be a writer, then this guide will also train you how.

Consequently, this guide has everything, and more than you can imagine. You can't even find all of this on YouTube because it is so intense and detailed that the videos would take so long to make. Instead, everything is at your fingertips, right here. What would take 20 hours of watching is condensed into three hours of reading. Unless you have won the lottery, this will be the most valuable three hours you've ever spent.

Mr Salles has dared to write a guide which will take you beyond the old A and A* grades. He urges you not just to dream of these grades, but to take action, take up your pen, and take charge. Dare to work hard, and deserve 100%. [483 words]

By now you ought to be able to spot all the techniques yourself!
You will notice that there is not much difference between writing to inform, and writing to persuade. The main difference is that the whole piece is presented as a series of facts. However, look closely, and you will see how much opinion is included with those facts.

Chapter 21: Recap

Reread the "bog standard" writing to inform, and then answer the questions below to see if you have nailed the skills of question 1 of paper 2.

Choose four statements that are true:

1. 1 million viewers have posted comments on Mr. Salles's YouTube channel.
2. Mr. Salles would sell more guides if he did not aim it at levels 4, 5 and 6.
3. Mr. Salles believes every student can understand some skills at levels 7, 8 and 9.
4. Mr. Salles believes every student can improve by reading this guide.
5. Mr. Salles believes every student will improve through practice.
6. Mr. Salles believes not every student can try to be excellent.
7. When examiners look for a "best fit" they expect your answer to have all of the skills of the level they award.
8. Mr. Salles encourages everyone reading this guide to post their attempts to him on his YouTube channel.

Answers:

1. **(F)** 1 million viewers have posted comments on Mr. Salles's YouTube channel.
2. **(F)** Mr. Salles would sell more guides if he did not aim it at levels 4, 5 and 6.
3. **(T)** Mr. Salles believes every student can understand some skills at levels 7, 8 and 9.
4. **(T)** Mr. Salles believes every student can improve by reading this guide.
5. **(T)** Mr. Salles believes every student will improve through practice.
6. **(F)** Mr. Salles believes not every student can try to be excellent.
7. **(F)** When examiners look for a "best fit" they expect your answer to have all of the skills of the level they award.
8. **(T)** Mr. Salles encourages everyone reading this guide to post their attempts to him on his YouTube channel.

"I am quite excited because the book I have been waiting for about mature male gorillas has just come out in silverback."
- Zoe Lyons

Chapter 22: How to Write Entertaining Texts

I have a secret hope, that after reading this, you will go to Project Guttenberg, and download all of Damon Runyon's stories, and that hundreds of you will write awesome American gangster based stories with the slang of 1920's New York in your GCSEs!

The Old Doll's House, by Damon Runyon

Now it seems that one cold winter night, a party of residents of Brooklyn comes across the Manhattan Bridge in an automobile wishing to pay a call on a guy by the name of Lance McGowan, who is well known to one and all along Broadway as a coming guy in the business world.

In fact, it is generally conceded that, barring accident, Lance will someday be one of the biggest guys in this country as an importer, and especially as an importer of such merchandise as fine liquors, because he is very bright, and has many good connections throughout the United States and Canada.

Furthermore, Lance McGowan is a nice-looking young guy and he has plenty of ticker, although some citizens say he does not show very sound business judgment in trying to move in on Angie the Ox over in Brooklyn, as Angie the Ox is an importer himself, besides enjoying a splendid trade in other lines, including artichokes and extortion.

Of course Lance McGowan is not interested in artichokes at all, and very little in extortion, but he does not see any reason why he shall not place his imports in a thriving territory such as Brooklyn, especially as his line of merchandise is much superior to anything handled by Angie the Ox.

Anyway, Angie is one of the residents of Brooklyn in the party that wishes to call on Lance McGowan, and besides Angie the party includes a guy by the name of Mockie Max, who is a very prominent character in Brooklyn, and another guy by the name of The Louse Kid, who is not so prominent, but who is considered a very promising young guy in many respects, although personally I think The Louse Kid has a very weak face.

He is supposed to be a wonderful hand with a burlap bag when anybody wishes to put somebody in such a bag, which is considered a great practical joke in Brooklyn, and in fact The Louse Kid has a burlap bag with him on the night in question, and they are figuring on putting Lance McGowan in the bag when they call on him, just for the laugh. Personally, I consider this a very crude form of humour, but then Angie the Ox and the other members of his party are very crude characters, anyway.

Well, it seems they have Lance McGowan pretty well cased, and they know that of an evening along toward ten o'clock he nearly always strolls through West Fifty-fourth street on his way to a certain spot on Park Avenue that is called the Humming Bird Club, which has a very high-toned clientele, and the reason Lance goes there is because he has a piece of the joint, and furthermore he loves to show off his shape in a tuxedo to the swell dolls.

So these residents of Brooklyn drive in their automobile along this route, and as they roll past Lance McGowan, Angie the Ox and Mockie Max let fly at Lance with a couple of sawed-offs, while The Louse Kid holds the burlap bag, figuring for all I know that Lance will be startled by the sawed-offs and will hop into the bag like a rabbit.

But Lance is by no means a sucker, and when the first blast of slugs from the sawed-offs breezes past him without hitting him, what does he do but hop over a brick wall alongside him and drop into a yard on the other side. So Angie the Ox, and Mockie Max and The Louse Kid get out of their automobile and run up close to the wall themselves because they commence figuring that if Lance McGowan starts popping at them from behind this wall, they will be taking plenty the worst of it, for of course they cannot figure Lance to be strolling about without being rodded up somewhat.

But Lance is by no means rodded up, because a rod is apt to create a bump in his shape when he has his tuxedo on, so the story really begins with Lance McGowan behind the brick wall, practically defenceless, and the reason I know this story is because Lance McGowan tells most of it to me, as Lance knows that I know his real name is Lancelot, and he feels under great obligation to me because I never mention the matter publicly.

Now, the brick wall Lance hops over is a wall around a pretty fair-sized yard, and the yard belongs to an old two-story stone house, and this house is well known to one and all in this man's town as a house of great mystery, and it is pointed out as such by the drivers of sightseeing buses.

This house belongs to an old doll by the name of Miss Abigail Ardsley, and anybody who ever reads the newspapers will tell you that Miss Abigail Ardsley has so many potatoes that it is really painful to think of, especially to people who have no potatoes whatever. In fact, Miss Abigail Ardsley has practically all the potatoes in the world, except maybe a few left over for general circulation.

These potatoes are left to her by her papa, old Waldo Ardsley, who accumulates same in the early days of this town by buying corner real estate very cheap before people realize this real estate will be quite valuable later on for fruit-juice stands and cigar stores.

It seems that Waldo is a most eccentric old bloke, and is very strict with his daughter, and will never let her marry, or even as much as look as if she wishes to marry, until finally she is so old she does not care a cuss about marrying, or anything else, and becomes very eccentric herself.

In fact, Miss Abigail Ardsley becomes so eccentric that she cuts herself off from everybody, and especially from a lot of relatives who are wishing to live off her, and any time anybody cuts themselves off from such characters they are considered very eccentric, indeed, especially by the relatives. She lives in the big house all alone, except for a couple of old servants, and it is very seldom that anybody sees her around and about, and many strange stories are told of her.

Well, no sooner is he in the yard than Lance McGowan begins looking for a way to get out, and one way he does not wish to get out is over the wall again, because he figures Angie the Ox and his sawed-offs are bound to be waiting for him in Fifty-fourth Street. So Lance looks around to see if there is some way out of the yard in another direction, but it seems there is no such way, and pretty soon he sees the snozzle of a sawed-off come poking over the wall, with the ugly kisser of Angie the Ox behind it, looking for him, and there is Lance McGowan all cornered up in the yard, and not feeling so good, at that.

Then Lance happens to try a door on one side of the house, and the door opens at once and Lance McGowan hastens in to find himself in the living room of the house. It is a very large living room with very nice furniture standing around and about, and oil paintings on the walls, and a big old grandfather's clock as high as the ceiling, and statuary here and there. In fact, it is such a nice, comfortable-looking room that Lance McGowan is greatly surprised, as he is expecting to find a regular mystery-house room such as you see in the movies, with cobwebs here and there, and everything all rotted up, and maybe Boris Karloff wandering about making strange noises.

But the only person in this room seems to be a little old doll all dressed in soft white, who is sitting in a low rocking-chair by an open fireplace in which a bright fire is going, doing some tatting.

Well, naturally Lance McGowan is somewhat startled by this scene, and he is figuring that the best thing he can do is to guzzle the old doll before she can commence yelling for the gendarmes, when she looks up at him and gives him a soft smile, and speaks to him in a soft voice, as follows:

'Good evening,' the old doll says.

Well, Lance cannot think of any reply to make to this at once, as it is certainly not a good evening for him, and he stands there looking at the old doll, somewhat dazed, when she smiles again and tells him to sit down.

So the next thing Lance knows, he is sitting there in a chair in front of the fireplace chewing the fat with the old doll as pleasant as you please, and of course the old doll is nobody but Miss Abigail Ardsley. Furthermore, she does not seem at all alarmed, or even much surprised, at seeing Lance in her house, but then Lance is never such a looking guy as is apt to scare old dolls, or young dolls either, especially when he is all slicked up.

Of course Lance knows who Miss Abigail Ardsley is, because he often reads stories in the newspapers about her the same as everybody else, and he always figures such a character must be slightly daffy to cut herself off from everybody when she has all the potatoes in the world, and there is so much fun going on, but he is very courteous to her, because after all he is a guest in her home.

'You are young.' the old doll says to Lance McGowan, looking him in the kisser. 'It is many years since a young man comes through yonder door. 'Ah, yes: she says, 'so many years.'

And with this she lets out a big sigh, and looks so very sad that Lance McGowan's heart is touched. 'Forty-five years now,' the old doll says in a low voice, as if she is talking to herself. 'So young, so handsome, and so good.'

And although Lance is in no mood to listen to reminiscences at this time, the next thing he knows he is hearing a very pathetic love story, because it seems that Miss Abigail Ardsley is once all hotted up over a young guy who is nothing but a clerk in her papa's office.

It seems from what Lance McGowan gathers that there is nothing wrong with the young guy that a million bobs will not cure, but Miss Abigail Ardsley's papa is a mean old waffle, and he will never listen to her having any truck with a poor guy, so they dast not let him know how much they love each other. But it seems that Miss Abigail Ardsley's ever-loving young guy has plenty of moxie, and every night he comes to see her after her papa goes to the hay, and she lets him in through the same side-door Lance McGowan comes through, and they sit by the fire and hold hands, and talk in low tones, and plan what they will do when the young guy makes a scratch.

Then one night it seems Miss Abigail Ardsley's papa has the stomach ache, or some such, and cannot sleep a wink, so he comes wandering downstairs looking for the Jamaica ginger, and catches Miss

Abigail Ardsley and her ever-loving guy in a clutch that will win the tide for any wrestler that can ever learn it.

Well, this scene is so repulsive to Miss Abigail Ardsley's papa that he is practically speechless for a minute, and then he orders the young guy out of his life in every respect, and tells him never to darken his door again, especially the side-door. But it seems that by this time a great storm is raging outside, and Miss Abigail Ardsley begs and pleads with her papa to let the young guy at least remain until the storm subsides, but between being all sored up at the clutching scene he witnesses, and his stomach ache, Mr. Ardsley is very hard-hearted, indeed, and he makes the young guy take the wind.

The next morning the poor young guy is found at the side-door frozen as stiff as a board, because it seems that the storm that is raging is the blizzard of 1888, which is a very famous event in the history of New York, although up to this time Lance McGowan never hears of it before, and does not believe it until he looks the matter up afterwards. It seems from what Miss Abigail Ardsley says that as near as anyone can make out, the young guy must return to the door seeking shelter after wandering about in the storm a while, but of course by this time her papa has the door all bolted up, and nobody hears the young guy.

'And,' Miss Abigail Ardsley says to Lance McGowan, after giving him all these details, 'I never speak to my papa again as long as he lives, and no other man ever comes in or out of yonder door, or any other door of this house, until your appearance to-night, although,' she says, 'this side-door is never locked in case such a young man comes seeking shelter.'

Then she looks at Lance McGowan in such a way that he wonders if Miss Abigail Ardsley hears the sawed-offs going when Angie the Ox and Mockie Max are tossing slugs at him, but he is too polite to ask.

Well, all these old-time memories seem to make Miss Abigail Ardsley feel very tough, and by and by she starts to weep, and if there is one thing Lance McGowan cannot stand it is a doll weeping, even if she is nothing but an old doll. So he starts in to cheer Miss Abigail Ardsley up, and he pats her on the arm, and says to her like this:

'Why,' Lance says, 'I am greatly surprised to hear your statement about the doors around here being so little used. Why, Sweetheart,' Lance says, 'if I know there is a doll as good-looking as you in the neighbourhood, and a door unlocked, I will be busting in myself every night. Come, come, come,' Lance says, 'let us talk things over and maybe have a few laughs, because I may have to stick around here a while. Listen, Sweetheart,' he says, 'do you happen to have a drink in the joint?'

Well, at this Miss Abigail Ardsley dries her eyes, and smiles again, and then she pulls a sort of rope near her, and in comes a guy who seems about ninety years old, and who seems greatly surprised to see Lance there. In fact, he is so surprised that he is practically tottering when he leaves the room after hearing Miss Abigail Ardsley tell him to bring some wine and sandwiches.

And the wine he brings is such wine that Lance McGowan has half a mind to send some of the lads around afterwards to see if there is any more of it in the joint, especially when he thinks of the unlocked side-door, because he can sell this kind of wine by the carat.

Well, Lance sits there with Miss Abigail Ardsley sipping wine and eating sandwiches, and all the time he is telling her stories of one kind and another, some of which he cleans up a little when he figures they may be a little too snappy for her, and by and by he has her laughing quite heartily indeed.
Finally he figures there is no chance of Angie and his sawed-offs being outside waiting for him, so he

says he guesses he will be going, and Miss Abigail Ardsley personally sees him to the door, and this time it is the front door, and as Lance is leaving he thinks of something he once sees a guy do on the stage, and he takes Miss Abigail Ardsley's hand and raises it to his lips and gives it a large kiss, all of which is very surprising to Miss Abigail Ardsley, but more so to Lance McGowan when he gets to thinking about it afterwards.

Just as he figures, there is no one in sight when he gets out in the street, so he goes on over to the Humming Bird Club, where he learns that many citizens are greatly disturbed by his absence, and are wondering if he is in The Louse Kid's burlap bag, for by this time it is pretty well known that Angie the Ox and his fellow citizens of Brooklyn are around and about.

In fact, somebody tells Lance that Angie is at the moment over in Good Time Charley's little speak in West Forty-ninth Street, buying drinks for one and all, and telling how he makes Lance McGowan hop a brick wall, which of course sounds most disparaging of Lance.

Well, while Angie is still buying these drinks, and still speaking of making Lance a brick-wall hopper, all of a sudden the door of Good Time Charley's speak opens and in comes a guy with a Betsy in his hand and this guy throws four slugs into Angie the Ox before anybody can say hello.

Furthermore, the guy throws one slug into Mockie Max, and one slug into The Louse Kid, who are still with Angie the Ox, so the next thing anybody knows there is Angie as dead as a door-nail, and there is Mockie Max even deader than Angie, and there is The Louse making a terrible fuss over a slug in his leg, and nobody can remember what the guy who plugs them looks like, except a couple of stool pigeons who state that the guy looks very much like Lance McGowan.

So what happens but early the next morning Johnny Brannigan, the plain-clothes copper, puts the arm on Lance McGowan for plugging Angie the Ox, and Mockie Max and The Louse Kid, and there is great rejoicing in copper circles generally because at this time the newspapers are weighing in the sacks on the coppers quite some, claiming there is too much lawlessness going on around and about and asking why somebody is not arrested for something.

So the collar of Lance McGowan is water on the wheel of one and all because Lance is so prominent, and anybody will tell you that it looks as if it is a sure thing that Lance will be very severely punished, and maybe sent to the electric chair, although he hires Judge Goldstein, who is one of the surest-footed lawyers in this town, to defend him. But even Judge Goldstein admits that Lance is in a tough spot, especially as the newspapers are demanding justice, and printing long stories about Lance, and pictures of him, and calling him some very uncouth names.

Finally Lance himself commences to worry about his predicament, although up to this time a little thing like being charged with murder in the first degree never bothers Lance very much. And in fact he will not be bothering very much about this particular charge if he does not find the D. A. very fussy about letting him out on bail. In fact, it is nearly two weeks before he lets Lance out on bail, and all this time Lance is in the sneezer, which is a most mortifying situation to a guy as sensitive as Lance. Well, by the time Lance's trial comes up, you can get 3 to 1 anywhere that he will be convicted, and the price goes up to 5 when the prosecution gets through with its case, and proves by the stool pigeons that at exactly twelve o'clock on the night of January 5th, Lance McGowan steps into Good Time Charley's little speak and plugs Angie the Ox, Mockie Max and The Louse Kid.

Furthermore, several other witnesses who claim they know Lance McGowan by sight testify that they see Lance in the neighbourhood of Good Time Charley's around twelve o'clock, so by the time it comes Judge Goldstein's turn to put on the defence, many citizens are saying that if he can do no more than beat the chair for Lance he will be doing a wonderful job.

Well, it is late in the afternoon when Judge Goldstein gets up and looks all around the courtroom, and without making any opening statement to the jury for the defence, as these mouthpieces usually do, he says like this:

'Call Miss Abigail Ardsley,' he says.

At first nobody quite realizes just who Judge Goldstein is calling for, although the name sounds familiar to one and all present who read the newspapers, when in comes a little old doll in a black silk dress that almost reaches the floor, and a black bonnet that makes a sort of a frame for her white hair and face.

Afterwards I read in one of the newspapers that she looks like she steps down out of an old-fashioned ivory miniature and that she is practically beautiful, but of course Miss Abigail Ardsley has so many potatoes that no newspaper dast to say she looks like an old chromo.

Anyway, she comes into the courtroom surrounded by so many old guys you will think it must be recess at the Old Men's Home, except they are all dressed up in claw-hammer coat tails, and high collars, and afterwards it turns out that they are the biggest lawyers in this town, and they all represent Miss Abigail Ardsley one way or another, and they are present to see that her interests are protected, especially from each other.

Nobody ever sees so much bowing and scraping before in a courtroom. In fact, even the judge bows, and although I am only a spectator I find myself bowing too, because the way I look at it, anybody with as many potatoes as Miss Abigail Ardsley is entitled to a general bowing. When she takes the witness-stand, her lawyers grab chairs and move up as close to her as possible, and in the street outside there is practically a riot as word goes around that Miss Abigail Ardsley is in the court, and citizens come running from every which way, hoping to get a peek at the richest old doll in the world.

Well, when all hands finally get settled down a little, Judge Goldstein speaks to Miss Abigail Ardsley as follows:

'Miss Ardsley,' he says, 'I am going to ask you just two or three questions. Kindly look at this defendant,' Judge Goldstein says, pointing at Lance McGowan, and giving Lance the office to stand up. 'Do you recognize him?'

Well, the little old doll takes a gander at Lance, and nods her head yes, and Lance gives her a large smile, and Judge Goldstein says:

'Is he a caller in your home on the night of January fifth?' Judge Goldstein asks.
'He is,' Miss Abigail Ardsley says.

'Is there a clock in the living-room in which you receive this defendant?' Judge Goldstein says.

'There is,' Miss Abigail Ardsley says. 'A large clock,' she says. 'A grandfather's clock.'

'Do you happen to notice,' Judge Goldstein says, 'and do you now recall the hour indicated by this clock when the defendant leaves your home?'

'Yes,' Miss Abigail Ardsley says, 'I do happen to notice. It is just twelve o'clock by my clock,' she says. 'Exactly twelve o'clock,' she says.

Well, this statement creates a large sensation in the courtroom, because if it is twelve o'clock when Lance McGowan leaves Miss Abigail Ardsley's house in West Fifty-fourth Street, anybody can see that there is no way he can be in Good Time Charley's little speak over five blocks away at the same minute unless he is a magician, and the judge begins peeking over his specs at the coppers in the courtroom very severe, and the cops begin scowling at the stool pigeons, and I am willing to lay plenty of 6 to 5 that the stools will wish they are never born before they hear the last of this matter from the gendarmes.

Furthermore, the guys from the D. A.'s office who are handling the prosecution are looking much embarrassed, and the jurors are muttering to each other, and right away Judge Goldstein says he moves that the case against his client be dismissed, and the judge says he is in favour of the motion, and he also says he thinks it is high time the gendarmes in this town learn to be a little careful who they are arresting for murder, and the guys from the D. A.'s office do not seem to be able to think of anything whatever to say.

So there is Lance as free as anybody, and as he starts to leave the courtroom he stops by Miss Abigail Ardsley, who is still sitting in the witness-chair surrounded by her mouthpieces, and he shakes her hand and thanks her, and while I do not hear it myself, somebody tells me afterwards that Miss Abigail Ardsley says to Lance in a low voice, like this:

'I will be expecting you again some night, young man,' she says.

'Some night, Sweetheart,' Lance says, 'at twelve o'clock.'

And then he goes on about his business, and Miss Abigail Ardsley goes on about hers; and everybody says it is certainly a wonderful thing that a doll as rich as Miss Abigail Ardsley comes forward in the interests of justice to save a guy like Lance McGowan from a wrong rap.

But of course it is just as well for Lance that Miss Abigail Ardsley does not explain to the court that when she recovers from the shock of the finding of her ever-loving young guy frozen to death, she stops all the clocks in her house at the hour she sees him last, so for forty-five years it is always twelve o'clock in her house.

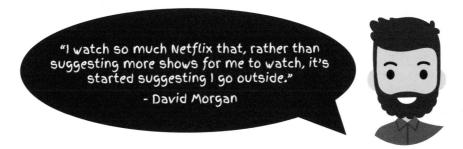

"I watch so much Netflix that, rather than suggesting more shows for me to watch, it's started suggesting I go outside."
- David Morgan

Features of writing to entertain:

An unusual premise. Here we are sympathetic to a murderer.

A clearly reconstructed world. Here 1920s New York during the time of the prohibition, in a society involving criminals and gangsters.

An interesting vocabulary. Here the choice of a specialist, slang register or argot.

Irony, where ideas are presented as facts, but where the opposite is intended to be understood to be true. Here "the party that wishes to call" actually wishes to kill. Similarly, putting someone in a burlap sack is "a very crude form of humour", in the sense that it is not funny at all, it kills the victim. "Good connections" who are clearly not good, but criminal: "because after all he is a guest in her home" when we know he is clearly an intruder.

A deliberate ending. Here, the ending also turns out to be ironic, as one crucial fact turns out to mean something entirely different when we get there. This is the detail of the clock being stuck at 12 o'clock.

The use of understatement: "any time anybody cuts themselves off from such characters they are considered very eccentric, indeed, especially by the relatives." They consider her much more than eccentric because she gives them none of her money.

"and there is Lance McGowan all cornered up in the yard, and not feeling so good, at that." He is terrified that he will be killed, not just "not feeling good".

Euphemism: "in the import business". This means smuggling illegal alcohol.

Hyperbole. "She has nearly all of the potatoes in the world."

Humorous comparisons. Simile. "He will hop into the bag like a rabbit".

Deliberate use of contrast to confound a character's, or our, expectations: "In fact, it is such a nice, comfortable-looking room that Lance McGowan is greatly surprised, as he is expecting to find a regular mystery-house room such as you see in the movies, with cobwebs here and there, and everything all rotted up, and maybe Boris Karloff wandering about making strange noises."

Write your own gangster-based story, and post it to me on YouTube. I will make you a video.

Why do pens get sent to prison to do?
Long sentences!

Chapter 23: Features of Writing to Advise

Many people ask, what is the purpose of education? The answer will determine what you choose at A level. If you know you have a career in mind, your choices are simpler. Usually these will involve the sciences and maths.

But what if you are artistic? Should you take A levels in drama, music or art? Well, to answer that, you need to consider what job you might get in the future. How many such students who get a degree in these subjects end up teaching? Many. How many end up in jobs where they don't use their subject all? Many more. Another factor to consider is the low income this will likely lead to. Not many artists or actors make a living at their craft.

However, there are advantages to following your passions, if you do so with your eyes open. What if you are prepared to spend till you are 28 pursuing your passion, to see if it will work out? 28 is not too late for a career change. Moreover, you will repay very little of your student loan, as payments don't start until you earn over £21,000. A passion for music, drama or art can also fulfil you for life: these are activities you never have to let go, even if later you do need to find a different way to make money.

In addition, the creative industries are growing faster than any other area of the UK economy. Fashion, music, animation, film - all might be an avenue for you. Trying till you are 28 gives you the best of both worlds, a calculated gamble with a half dozen years you can afford to invest in yourself.

Alternatively, you might want to look at most likely scenarios. If you take a look at the most employable degree subjects, you will find them dominated by sciences and maths. Should you take these subjects simply because financial security lies ahead? The simple answer is no. A life devoid of passion is no life at all. Look around at you at the adults in jobs they dislike. Do you want that to be you? Does their financial security make them happy?

So, if science and maths are subjects you don't enjoy, will any degree do? Yes, and no. Your degree is a passport to your future provided you get at least a 2:1. Next you must consider the university itself. Which ones are more marketable? Where you have a choice, pick the university that demands the highest grades. But, in a world where being a teaching assistant is considered a graduate job, is the degree enough? Do you run the risk of being poorly paid? Should you therefore skip university altogether and simply enter the world of work? Hotel management, sales, retail management, banking, accountancy?

Here your choices are more difficult. Yes, when only 15-20% of students took degrees, having a degree led to greater lifetime earnings, often much greater. This was a no brainer. But now, when nearly 50% of 22 year olds have a degree, future earnings are less certain. About 70% of graduates are not predicted to earn enough to repay their loans. Is a degree too likely to be a financial burden?

No. this is the wrong way to look at its cost. Instead, this figure is exciting - it means that a university degree is value for money - like only paying 70% of the cost of your holiday. You are actually getting your degree on the cheap. Will graduates still earn more than non-graduates? Very probably. If you are an employer, why would you choose someone less qualified?

But there is another factor we haven't considered, that has only a little to do with your employability, and only a little to do with the subject you study. The other factor is you. University will make you. All the mistakes you will make between 18 and 21 will be made away from home. Emotionally, they will cost you much less. Don't underestimate this - families and parents have very long memories indeed!

In these three or four university years you will probably change as much as you did in the whole of your time at secondary school. You will meet new ways of thinking, of behaving, of being. You will literally find out who you are. More than this, you will form lifetime friendships in a way that jobs don't. You are very likely to meet your future husband or wife at university. You will think nothing of travelling the world. Not only will you meet people to do this with, whatever stage in your life you devote to travel, you will find people you know, or their families, already living abroad, ready to welcome you and even offer you work.

So, my final advice, no matter what your passion, what your subject, is the argument for personal growth. Find out who you are going to be. Find yourself at university. [828 words]

The full stop had been stuffing itself all year. It was now a very full stop indeed.

"Doctor, what can you do for me?" asked the full stop.

"We'll fit you with a gastric band," she said.

After the operation, the full stop looked in the mirror: "damn, I'm a semi-colon."

Features of advisory writing:

Read through the text again, and see if you can spot where the following techniques are. (If I showed you, how would you know you were learning from the guide?)

Language Features:
- Use of facts and statistics
- Written in the second person
- Lots of rhetorical techniques (like those listed in our mnemonic MAD FATHERS CROCH)
- Use of contrast
- Reassuring tone
- Conditional language, to show that things are not certain, and the future is not certain

Structural Features:
- Alternative viewpoints
- Connectives to show balanced perspectives
- Repetition for emphasis
- Ask and answer questions
- The best arguments are put last
- A punchy conclusion

Chapter 24: Structure

When thinking about the structure of a text, there are only two questions to ask:

- Why has the writer revealed things in this order?
- Why has it been revealed in this way?

The order is always connected to how hard the writer wants to make you work. In fiction, the writer will encourage you to make predictions, so they drop continual clues about what might happen next. Often these will be false clues, to create a sense of suspense. At other times, they will confront you with details you might not want to know, especially when dealing with tragic events.

Conversely, in persuasive or argumentative writing, the opposite occurs: the structure will try to stop you thinking for yourself. Thus, facts and arguments will be revealed in an order that builds in strength, towards a conclusion that acts as a climax. The whole point of the text is to carry you to a conclusion so that you can't possibly disagree with it.

To analyse the way things are revealed, you ask yourself how things are emphasised. For example:

- To increase their importance, repetition, emotive language, triplets, and hyperbole are typically used.
- To decrease or minimise their importance, analogy, humour, and rhetorical questions tend to be used.

It is important to realise, though, that all rhetorical techniques can be used either to emphasise or to minimise (provide less emphasis).

So, when writing about the effect of structure, you are writing about how the author controls the reader' emotions and ideas. When looked at this way, I hope you will feel that it is not complex. It will help if we look at a text entirely in terms of its structure, so you can see how this works. Let's look again at my advisory text about whether you should go to university. We will analyse each paragraph in terms of its part in the structure of the whole text.

- The first paragraph sets out what the issue is and why the reader should pay attention to it.

Many people ask, what is the purpose of education? The answer will determine what you choose at A level. If you know you have a career in mind, your choices are simpler. Usually these will involve the sciences and maths.

- The repetition of questions anticipates the worries readers might have about the issue.
- Repetition is used to emphasise the writer's superior knowledge and position as an expert.

But what if you are artistic? Should you take A levels in drama, music or art? Well, to answer that, you need to consider what job you might get in the future. How many such students get a degree in these subjects end up teaching? Many. How many end up in jobs where they don't use their subject all? Many more. Another factor to consider is the low income this will likely lead to. Not many artists or actors make a living at their craft.

- The connective signals a counter argument.
- The purpose of the counter argument is to show how the writer has considered all possible advantages and disadvantages of the issue.
- The final sentence offers a balanced solution.

However, there are advantages to following your passions, if you do so with your eyes open. What if you are prepared to spend till you are 28 pursuing your passion, to see if it will work out? 28 is not too late for a career change. Moreover, you will repay very little of your student loan, as payments don't start until you earn over £21,000. A passion for music, drama or art can also fulfil you for life: these are activities you never have to let go, even if you do need to find a way to make money later.

- The next paragraph gives more detail about that balanced solution. Facts are included to make this the advice of an expert.

In addition, the creative industries are growing faster than any other area of the UK economy. Fashion, music, animation, film - all might be an avenue for you. Trying till you are 28 gives you the best of both worlds, a calculated gamble with a half dozen years you can afford to invest in yourself.

- This paragraph anticipates readers who are still not convinced. It predicts their arguments in order to counter them.
- Setting these up as a question at the end of the paragraph allows the advice of the subsequent paragraph to be more forceful: it will provide the answer.

Alternatively, you might want to look at the most likely of scenarios. If you take a look at the most employable degree subjects, you will find them dominated by sciences and maths. Should you take these subjects simply because financial security lies ahead?

- The advice is made more forceful through the use of imperative verbs.
- Listing rhetorical questions has the same forceful effect.

The simple answer is no. A life devoid of passion is no life at all. Look around at you at the adults in jobs they dislike. Do you want that to be you? Does their financial security make them happy?

- In order not to browbeat or bully the reader, the next two paragraphs introduce a new problem. This again anticipates readers' counter arguments.

So, if science and maths are subjects you don't enjoy, will any degree do? Yes, and no. Your degree is a passport to your future provided you get at least a 2:1. Next you must consider the university itself. Which ones are more marketable? Where you have a choice, pick the university that demands the highest grades.

But, in a world where being a teaching assistant is considered a graduate job, is this enough? Do you run the risk of being poorly paid? Should you therefore skip university altogether and simply enter the world of work? Hotel management, sales, retail management, banking, accountancy?

- The use of facts and statistics here tells the reader that the solution will be based on sound reasoning rather than emotion.
- This pretends that the writer's opinion is the only valid opinion.

Here your choices are more difficult. Yes, when only 15-20% of students took degrees, having a degree led to greater lifetime earnings, often much greater. This was a no brainer. But now, when nearly 50% of 22 year olds have a degree, future earnings are less certain. About 70% of graduates are not predicted to earn enough to repay their loans. Is a degree too likely to be a financial burden?

- The rhetorical questions in this paragraph emphasise that the writer's opinions are impossible to argue with. The reader is simply invited to agree.

No. this is the wrong way to look at its cost. Instead, this is exciting - it means that a university degree is value for money - like only paying 70% of the cost of your holiday. You are actually getting your degree on the cheap. Will graduates still earn more than non-graduates? Most probably. If you are an employer, why would you choose someone less qualified?

- The conclusion is set up as a revelation. The final argument is revealed as a surprise. It suggests that the writer has thought much more deeply about this issue than the reader has, again demanding that the reader accept the writer's advice.
- The final sentence of this paragraph also warns of the dangers of not heeding this advice.

But there is another factor we haven't considered, that has only a little to do with your employability, and only a little to do with the subject you study. The other factor is you. University will make you. All the mistakes you will make between 18 and 21 will be made away from home. Emotionally, they will cost you much less. Don't underestimate this, families and parents have very long memories indeed!

- The repetition in this paragraph emphasises the many advantages of accepting the writer's advice.
- The continual direct address also personalises these advantages.
- The conclusion tries to be as broad as possible, not just looking at future events, but also the broader world. This emphasises the breadth of opportunity which following this advice will unlock.

In these three or four years you will probably change as much as you did in the whole of your time at secondary school. You will meet new ways of thinking, of behaving, of being. You will literally find out who you are. More than this, you will form lifetime friendships in a way that jobs don't. You are very likely to meet your future husband or wife at university. You will think nothing of travelling the world. Not only will you meet people to do this with, whatever stage in your life you devote to travel, you will find people you know, or their families, already living abroad, ready to welcome you and even offer you work.

- The concluding paragraph is deliberately brief in order to cut down the reader's thinking and choice.
- The imperative verbs, and their repetition, emphasise what the reader must do: accept the writer's advice.

So, my final advice, no matter what your passion, what your subject, is the argument for personal growth. Find out who you are going to be. Find yourself at university.
Now I hope you can see that every paragraph has a structural purpose you can comment on. These are easy to find once you practise thinking in this way.
My sentences also model how you should write about structure. You always write about what is emphasised. You always link this to the writer's purpose. That's it!

My Grandad had a heart attack on the ski slopes.

After that, he went downhill fast.

Still, my family said, it's what he would have wanted.

But I'm not so sure, he was going to take up snowboarding.

Chapter 25: Features of 19th Century Non-Fiction

19th century letters are full of strong emotion. Friendships were maintained in this way, in an era where distances still required time and effort to cover.

The act of writing was also much slower, due to the need to continually dip a quill in ink. This naturally leads to more crafted letters. Writers choose both better vocabulary and much more complex sentences, where extra ideas and information are added clause by clause, necessitating the use of commas in parenthesis (and, of course, the ever present brackets).

As you can see, I have deliberately written this paragraph in the same style, so that you might feel how it works (a practice I encourage you to try for yourself) and thereby experience crafting sentences like Dickens.

Long, complex, clause-filled sentences
Use of **superlatives**
Personal connection to the recipient
Formal tone: sir is used, as well as my dear
In order to bring places and people to life, **well-chosen adjectives**, often in **pairs**
Verbs also are listed in pairs, to add drama and emphasis
The writer is likely to **ask questions** to elicit news from the recipient, and also share news about themselves, **often revealing their emotions**
Often, the purpose will be to entertain as well as inform.
The structure may not feel planned, as new thoughts are added, although it is very likely to be **chronologically sequenced.**
Often there are likely to be requests for action, **a call to action**, especially towards the end.

See if you can spot these features in the letter from Dickens, below:

From Charles Dickens

"My dear Cerjat,

So wonderfully do good (epistolary) intentions become confounded with bad execution, that I assure you I laboured under a perfect and most comfortable conviction that I had answered your Christmas Eve letter of 1855. More than that, in spite of your assertions to the contrary, I still strenuously believe that I did so! I have more than half a mind ("Little Dorrit" and my other occupations notwithstanding) to charge you with having forgotten my reply!! I have even a wild idea that Townshend reproached me, when the last old year was new, with writing to you instead of to him!!! We will argue it out, as well as we can argue anything without poor dear Haldimand, when I come back to Elysée. In any case, however, don't discontinue your annual letter, because it has become an expected and a delightful part of the season to me."

A synoynm ambles into a pub. She's accompanied by a piece of string. The barman says, "I hope you're not a piece of string, we don't serve string." "No," replies the string, "I'm a frayed knot."

Chapter 26: High Frequency Spelling Mistakes

High frequency spelling mistakes of students seeking an A Grade (Level 7)
High frequency words are in bold

- Absolutely
- Allowance
- Allowed
- Always
- Balconies
- Believable
- Believe
- Completely
- Disappeared
- Emphasise
- Especially
- Excited
- Excitement
- Exciting
- Families
- Focuses
- Government
- Imaginable
- Imagine
- Immediately
- Interested
- Intrigued
- Opinion
- Pleasurable
- Reference
- Referring
- Rehearsed
- Simile
- Surprise
- Travelled
- Unbelievable

Typical Spelling Mistakes From Students Aspiring to A Grade in their mocks

- 1940s
- A bit
- A lot
- Abnormalities
- Absences
- **9. Absolutely**
- Academic
- Acceptable
- Accommodation
- Aggressive
- **10. Allowance**
- **11. allowed**
- Already
- **12. Always**
- American
- leisure
- Rapunzel
- Anecdote
- Apartments
- Apparently
- Appointments
- Approaching
- Argument
- Associated
- Audience
- Awakening
- **13. Balconies**
- Barbados
- Beginning
- Behaviour
- **14. Believable**
- **15. Believe**
- Benefits
- Bravado
- British
- Capable
- Charcoal
- Cigarettes
- Companion
- **16. Completely**
- Concentrates
- Consistency
- Continuously
- Contradicts
- Contrasts
- Crowd
- Decisions
- Definitely
- Destinations
- Different
- **17. Disappeared**
- Doesn't
- Dominance
- Earrings

- Eats
- Emotion
18. **Emphasise**
- Encouraging
- Envision
19. **Especially**
- Exaggerated
20. **Excited**
21. **Excitement**
22. **Exciting**
- Experience
- Extraordinary
23. **Families**
- Famous
24. **Focuses**
- Fondly
- Fortunately
- Frantically
- Geography
25. **Government**
- Happened
- He's
- Hobbling
- Holidays
- Humidity
- Hyperbole
26. **Imaginable**
27. **Imagine**
28. **Immediately**
- Immense
- Implies
- Inadvertently
- Inhabitants
- Integrated

- Intellectual
29. **Interested**
- Intimidating
30. **Intrigued**
- Isn't
- Luckily
- Magnificent
- Majestic
- Malicious
- Manliness
- Metaphor
- Monstrosity
- Mountainous
- Obliged
- Obviously
- Occurrence
- Old fashioned
- unnecessary
31. **Opinion**
- Partial
- Pathetic fallacy
- Peacefulness
32. **Pleasurable**
- Positive
- Possibly
- Probably
- Quiet
33. **Reference**
34. **Referring**
35. **Rehearsed**
- released
- Repetition
- Reputation
- Restaurant

- Scenery
- Senior
- Sentences
- Separated
- She's
- Shiny
36. **Simile**
- Sophisticated
- Speech
- Statement
- Succeed
37. **Surprise**
- Surrounding
- Suspense
- Suspicious
- Technique
- That's
- Themselves
- Traffic
38. **Travelled**
- Treasures
39. **Unbelievable**
- Unnecessary
- Urgently
- Usually
- Vibrant
- Villages
- Visualise
- Whereas
- Whether
- Worries
- You're

High Frequency Words from my Guide

(This are all the words that appear frequently in the guide you have just read. This is a good indicator of spellings **you must know** in order to be sure of getting **level 8**)

4. **absolutely**
- academic
- accept
- accounts

- accuracy
- achieve
- acquaintance
- activities

- address
- adjectives
- advantage
- adventures

- adverb
- advice
- affect
- alarming
- allusion
- alternative
- although
- ambitious
- anecdote
- annoyance
- antagonists
- apparent
- appear
- approach
- appropriate
- argument
- article
- assess
- assonance
- assume
- athlete
- atmosphere
- attain
- attempt
- attention
- attention
- attractions
- audience
- author

5. **beautiful**
- because
- beginning
- believe
- beneath
- beyond
- boredom
- building

6. **candidates**
- celebrate
- century
- century

- challenge
- channel
- chapter
- character
- checklist
- childhood
- choice
- choose
- chronologically
- clamour
- clause
- close
- colon
- comma
- comparison
- comparison
- complete
- comprehensive
- conclusion
- confidence
- conflict
- confound
- connected
- connective
- consider
- contain
- context
- continue
- contrast
- conversely
- convince
- correct
- create
- crisis

7. **danger**
- daughter
- decide
- definitely
- deliberate
- demands
- describe
- description

- detail
- develop
- diamond
- difference
- direction
- disadvantages
- disagree
- disaster
- discuss
- dismissed
- display
- distance
- dog
- dramatic
- dream
- drive

8. **earlier**
- easy
- education
- effect
- embedded
- emotion
- emphasis
- emphasise
- encourage
- ending
- enjoy
- entertain
- escape
- eulogy
- evaluate
- examiner
- excellent
- exemplar
- expectation
- experience
- expert
- explanation
- exposition

9. **face**
- facts

- family
- fashion
- fathers
- features
- feeling
- fiction
- flavour
- fluent
- focused
- focuses
- force
- foreshadowing
- forgiveness
- formal
- future

10. **gangster**
- gendarmes
- Goldilocks
- grades
- grammar
- groan
- guide
- handwriting
- heart
- home
- homework
- hour
- humour
- hyperbole

11. **idea**
- illuminated
- imagery
- imitate
- implies
- important
- impossible
- improve
- Include
- increase
- indicate
- inference

- influence
- information
- insight
- Instagram
- Instead
- intelligence
- interesting
- interpretation
- introduce

12. **juxtaposition**

13. **language**
- laugh
- learning
- learning
- lesson
- like
- limit
- list
- load
- looking

14. **male**
- mark
- master
- masterpieces
- meaning
- memories
- metaphor
- minute
- mistake
- mother
- motion
- murder

15. **narrative**
- non-fiction
- notice
- novel

16. **objective**
- obsessed
- obviously

- occurred
- olympics
- onomatopoeia
- opening
- opinion
- oppose
- organisation
- original

17. **paragraph**
- paraphrase
- passages
- passion
- perceptive
- perhaps
- personification
- persuade
- photograph
- phrase
- picture
- planning
- plot
- portray
- power
- practice
- predict
- prepare
- pressure
- probably
- prohibition
- promise
- public
- punctuation
- purpose

18. **question**
- quotation

19. **reader**
- realise
- recreate
- references
- remember

- remind
- repetition
- resolution
- response
- reveal
- revision

20. **sample**
- scheme
- Scrooge
- selection
- sense
- sentence
- sexism
- sibilance
- signal
- significance
- similarly
- simile
- skill
- society
- solution
- sound
- standing

- start
- statement
- statistics
- stopping
- strike
- structure
- student
- success
- suggests
- summarise
- suppose
- surprise
- symbolism
- synthesise

21. **taste**
- teach
- technique
- teenager
- terminology
- text
- therefore
- think
- thoughts

- threatening
- through
- tongue
- topic
- trust

22. **understand**
- university

23. **verb**
- viewpoint
- visual

24. **whatever**
- windows
- women
- words
- writer
- writing

25. **year**
- yourself
- YouTube

Notes